DESERT FLOWER

The Extraordinary Life
of a Desert Nomad

WARIS DIRIE
and Cathleen Miller

virago

VIRAGO

First published by Virago Press in 1998
This edition published by Virago Press in 2001
Reprinted 2001, 2002 (twice), 2003, 2005, 2006, 2007 (twice),
2008, 2009 (twice), 2010 (twice), 2011, 2012 (twice), 2013, 2014

First published in the United States by
William Morrow and Company Inc., New York

A CIP catalogue record for this book
is available from the British Library.

ISBN 978-1-86049-758-2

Printed and bound in Great Britain by
Clays Ltd, St Ives plc

Papers used by Virago are from well-managed forests
and other responsible sources.

MIX
Paper from
responsible sources
FSC
www.fsc.org FSC® C104740

Virago Press
An imprint of
Little, Brown Book Group
100 Victoria Embankment
London EC4Y 0DY

An Hachette UK Company
www.hachette.co.uk

www.virago.co.uk

FOR MAMA

I realize that when one travels the road of life, weathering storms, enjoying the sunshine, standing in the eye of many hurricanes, survival is determined only by the strength of one's will. Therefore I dedicate this book to the woman upon whose shoulders I stand, whose strength is unyielding: my mother, Fattuma Ahmed Aden.

She has shown her children evidence of faith while staring into the face of unthinkable adversity. She has balanced an equal devotion to twelve children (an amazing feat on its own) and shown wisdom that would humble the most insightful sage.

Her sacrifices have been many; her complaints, few. And all along we, her children, knew that she gave what she had, no matter how meager—without reservation. She has known the agony of losing a child more than once, and still she maintains her strength and courage to continue struggling for her remaining children. Her generosity of spirit and inner and outer beauty are legendary.

Mama, I love, respect, and cherish you, and thank Almighty Allah for giving me you as my mother. My prayer is to honor your legacy by parenting my son as you have tirelessly nurtured your children.

Oh, you are a kilt which a young dandy set out to choose
Oh, you are like a costly rug for which thousands were paid
Will I ever find your like—you who have been shown to me
    only once?
An umbrella comes apart; you are as strong as looped iron;

Oh, you who are as the gold of Nairobi, finely molded,
You are the risen sun, and the early rays of dawn,
Will I ever find your like, you who have been shown to me only
   once?

—*Traditional Somali poem*

AUTHORS' NOTE

Desert Flower is the true story of Waris Dirie's life, and all the events presented are factual, based on Waris's recollection. While all the people portrayed in *Desert Flower* are real, we have used pseudonyms for most of them to protect their privacy.

DESERT FLOWER

1.

RUNNING AWAY

A slight sound woke me, and when I opened my eyes, I was staring into the face of a lion. Riveted awake, my eyes stretched wide—very wide—as if to expand enough to contain the animal in front of me. I tried to stand up, but I hadn't eaten for several days, so my weak legs wobbled and folded beneath me. Collapsing, I slumped back against the tree where I had been resting, sheltered from the African desert sun that becomes so merciless at noon. I quietly leaned my head back and closed my eyes, and felt the rough bark of the tree pressing into my skull. The lion was so near I could smell his musty scent in the hot air. I spoke to Allah: "It's the end for me, my God. Please take me now."

My long journey across the desert had come to an end. I had no protection, no weapon. Nor the strength to run. Even under the best of circumstances, I knew I couldn't beat the lion up the tree, because like all cats, lions with their strong claws are excellent climbers. By the time I got halfway up—BOOM— one swipe and I'd be gone. Without any fear I opened my eyes again and said to the lion, "Come and get me. I'm ready for you."

He was a beautiful male with a golden mane and a long tail switching back and forth to flick away flies. He was five or six years old, young and healthy. I knew he could crush me instantly; he was the king. All my life I'd watched those paws take down wildebeest and zebras weighing hundreds of pounds more than me.

The lion stared at me and slowly blinked his honey-colored eyes. My brown eyes stared back, locked on his. He looked away. "Go on. Take me now." He looked at me again, then looked away. He licked his lips and sat down on his haunches. Then the lion rose and paced back and forth in front of me, sexily, elegantly. Finally, he turned and walked away, no doubt deciding that I had so little flesh on my bones, I wasn't worth eating. He strode across the desert until his tawny-colored fur was lost against the sand.

When I realized he was not going to kill me, I gave no sigh of relief, because I hadn't been afraid. I'd been ready to die. But evidently God, who has always been my best friend, had something else planned, some reason to keep me alive. I said, "What is it? Take me—direct me," and struggled to my feet.

This nightmare journey began because I was running away from my father. I was about thirteen at the time, and living with my family, a tribe of nomads in the Somalian desert, when my father announced he had arranged my marriage to an old man. Knowing I had to act fast or suddenly one day my new husband would come to get me, I told my mother I wanted to run away. My plan was to find my aunt, my mother's sister, who lived in Mogadishu, the capital of Somalia. Of course I had never been to Mogadishu—or any other city for that matter. Nor had I ever met my aunt. But with the optimism of a child, I felt somehow things would magically work out.

While my father and the rest of the family were still sleeping, my mother woke me and said, "Go now." I looked around for something to grab, something to take, but there was nothing, no bottle of water, no jar of milk, no basket of food. So, barefoot, and wearing only a scarf draped around me, I ran off into the black desert night.

I didn't know which direction led to Mogadishu, so I just ran. Slowly at first, because I couldn't see; I stumbled along, tripping over roots. Finally, I decided to just sit down because snakes are everywhere in Africa, and I was terrified of snakes. Each root I stepped on I imagined to be the back of a spitting cobra. I sat watching the sky gradually lighten. Even before the sun came up—*whoosh*—I was off like a gazelle. I ran and I ran and I ran for hours.

By midday I'd traveled deep into the red sand, and deep into my own thoughts. Where in the hell was I going? I wondered. I didn't even know what direction I was heading in. The landscape stretched on to eternity, the sand broken only occasionally by an acacia or thorn tree; I could see for miles and miles. Hungry, thirsty, and tired, I slowed down and walked. Strolling along in a bored daze, I wondered where my new life would take me. What was going to happen next?

As I pondered these questions, I thought I heard a voice: "W-A-R-I-S . . .W-A-R-I-S. . . ." My father was calling me! Whipping around in circles, I looked for him, but saw no one. Maybe I was imagining things, I thought. "W-A-R-I-S . . . W-A-R-I-S . . ." the voice echoed all around me. The tone was pleading, but I was frightened all the same. If he caught me, he would surely take me back and make me marry that man, and probably beat me besides. I was not hearing things; it was my father, and he was getting closer. In earnest now, I started to run as fast as I could. Even though I had gotten a head start of several hours, Papa had caught up with me. As I later realized, he'd tracked me down by following my footprints through the sand.

My father was too old to catch me—so I had thought—because I was young and fast. To my childish thinking, he was an old man. Now I recall with a laugh that at the time, he was only in his thirties. We were all incredibly fit, because we ran everywhere; we had no car, no public transportation of any kind. And always I was fast, chasing the animals, heading after water, racing the oncoming darkness to reach home safely before the light was lost.

After a while I didn't hear my father calling my name anymore, so I slowed down to a jog. If I kept moving, Papa would get tired and go back home, I reasoned. Suddenly I looked back toward the horizon and saw him coming over the hill behind me. He'd spotted me, too. Terrified, I ran faster. And faster. It was as if we were surfing waves of sand; I flew up one hill, and he glided down the one behind me. On and on we continued for hours, until eventually I realized I hadn't seen him for some time. He no longer called out to me.

My heart pounding, finally I stopped, hiding behind a bush, and looked around. Nothing. I listened closely. No sound. When I came across a flat rock outcropping, I stopped to rest. But I'd learned from my mistake the night before, and when I began to run again, I went along the rocks where the ground was hard, then changed my direction so my father couldn't follow my footprints.

Papa, I reasoned, had turned around to try to make it back home, because now the sun was setting. Still, he would never make it back before the light faded. He'd have to run back through the darkness, listening for the night-time sounds of our family, tracing his path by the voices of children screaming, laughing, the animal noises of the herds mooing, bleating. The wind carries sounds great distances across the desert, so these noises acted as a lighthouse when we were lost in the night.

After walking along the rocks, I changed my direction. It didn't really matter what direction I chose, since I had no idea which was the right one to lead me to Mogadishu. I kept running until the sun set, the light was gone, and the night was so black I couldn't see. By this time I was starving, and food was all I could think about. My feet were bleeding. I sat down to rest under a tree and fell asleep.

In the morning, the sun burning my face woke me. I opened my eyes and looked up at the leaves of a beautiful eucalyptus tree stretching to the sky. Slowly the reality of my circumstances came to me. *My God, I'm all alone. What am I going to do?*

I got up and continued to run; for days I managed to keep it up. How many days, I'm not sure. All I know is that for me, there was no time; there was only hunger, thirst, fear, pain. When the evening grew too dark to see, I would stop and rest. At midday, when the sun was at its hottest, I would sit under a tree and take a siesta.

It was during one of these siestas that I fell asleep and the lion woke me. By this point I no longer cared about my freedom; I simply wanted to go back home to Mama. What I wanted more than food or water was my mother. And even though it was common for us to go for a day or two without food or water, I knew I couldn't survive much longer. I was so weak that I could barely move, and my feet were so cracked and sore that each step was agony. By the time the lion sat in front of me licking his lips in hunger, I had given up. I welcomed his quick kill as a way out of my misery.

But the lion looked at the bones jutting out of my skin, my sunken cheeks and bulging eyes, and walked away. I don't know if he took pity on such a miserable soul, or if it was simply a pragmatic decision that I wouldn't even make a worthy snack. Or if God had interceded on my behalf. But I decided God wouldn't be so heartless as to spare me, simply to let me die in some other, crueler way, like starving to death. He had another plan in store for me, so I called out for his guidance: "Take me—direct me." Holding on to the tree to steady myself, I rose to my feet and called out for his help.

I began to walk again, and within a few minutes came to a grazing area with camels everywhere. I spotted the animal carrying the most fresh milk, and ran to it. I nursed, sucking the milk like a baby. The herdsman spotted me and yelled out, "Get out of there, you little bitch!" and I heard a bullwhip crack. But I was desperate, and kept right on sucking, draining the milk as fast as my mouth could take it.

The herdsman ran at me, yelling, loud and mean. He knew that if he didn't scare me away, by the time he reached me, it would be too late. The milk would all be gone. But I'd had plenty, so I started to run. He chased after me, and managed to lash me with the whip a couple of times before I outran him. But I was faster than he was, and left him behind me, standing in the sand, cursing in the afternoon sun.

Now I had fuel in me; I was energized. So I kept running and running until I came to a village. I had never been in a place like this before; it had buildings, and streets made from hard-packed dirt. I walked down the middle of the street, just assuming this was the spot for me to walk. As I strolled through town, gawking at the strange setting, my head swiveled in every direction. A woman passed by me, looked me up and down, then called out: "You are so stupid. Where do you think you are?" To some of the other villagers walking down the street, she cried, "Oh, my goodness. Look at her feet!" She pointed at my feet, cracked and caked with bloody scabs. "Eh! Oh, my God. She must be a stupid little country girl." She knew. This woman yelled out to me, "Little girl, if you want to live, get off the street. Get off the road!" She waved me to the side, then laughed.

I knew everybody heard, and I was so embarrassed. I just hung my head down, but continued to walk in the middle of the road, because I didn't understand what she was talking about. Pretty soon, along came a truck. BEEP! BEEP! And I had to jump out of the way. I turned around to face the traffic, and as the cars and trucks headed toward me, I stuck out my hand. I can't say I was hitchhiking, because I didn't even know what hitchhiking was. So I just stood in the road with my hand stuck out to try and get someone to stop. A car careened past and nearly chopped my hand off, so I jerked it in. I thrust my hand out again, but this time not quite as far, moved a little farther to the side of the road, and kept walking. I looked into the faces of the people driving past me in their cars, silently praying for one of them to stop and help me.

Eventually a truck stopped. I am not proud of what happened next—but it happened, so what can I say, but to tell the truth? To this day, whenever I think of that truck stopping, I wish I had trusted my instincts and not gotten in.

The truck was hauling a load of stones for construction; they were jagged and the size of softballs. In front were two men; the driver opened the door and said in Somali, "Hop on, darling." I felt helpless, sick with fear.

"I'm headed to Mogadishu," I explained.

"I'll take you wherever you want to go," he said, grinning. When he smiled, his teeth showed red, tobacco red. But I knew that what made them that color wasn't tobacco, because I'd seen my father chew it once. It was khat, a narcotic plant the men in Africa chew that's similar to cocaine. Women are not allowed to touch it, and it's just as well; it makes the men crazy, overexcited, aggressive, and has destroyed many lives.

I knew I was in trouble, but I also didn't know what else to do, so I nodded. The driver told me to climb in the back. This brought me some relief, the thought of being away from the two men. I climbed into the truck bed and sat down in one corner, trying to make myself comfortable on the pile of rocks. It was dark now, and cool in the desert; as the truck started moving I was cold and lay down out of the wind.

The next thing I knew, the man riding with the driver was

next to me, kneeling on the stones. He was in his forties, and ugly, ugly. He was so ugly, his hair was leaving him; he was going bald. But he'd tried to make up for this fact by growing a little mustache. His teeth were chipped and some were missing; the remaining ones were stained a nasty red with the khat, but still he grinned at me, proudly displaying them. No matter how long I live, I will never forget his face leering at me.

He was also fat, as I learned when he took his pants down. His erect penis bobbed at me as he grabbed my legs and tried to force them apart.

"Oh, please, please, no," I begged. I wrapped my skinny legs around each other like pretzels and locked them shut. He grappled with me and tried to force them apart. Then, as he wasn't successful with this attempt, he drew back his hand and slapped me hard across the face. I let out a shrill scream that the air carried away as the truck sped into the night.

"OPEN YOUR FUCKING LEGS!" We struggled, with all his weight on top of me, the rough stones cutting into my back. He hauled back his hand and slapped me again, this time harder. With the second slap I knew I had to think of some other tactic; he was too strong for me to fight. This man obviously knew what he was doing. Unlike me, he was experienced, no doubt raping many women; I was simply about to become the next one. I deeply, deeply wanted to kill him, but I had no weapon.

So I pretended to want him. I said sweetly, *"Okay, okay.* But first let me pee-pee." I could see he was growing even more excited now—hey, this little girl wanted him!—and he let me up. I went to the opposite corner of the truck and pretended to squat and pee in the darkness. This bought me a few minutes to think of what to do next. By the time I finished my little charade, I had formed my plan. I picked up the largest stone I could find and, holding it in my hand, went back and lay down beside him.

He climbed on top of me and I squeezed the stone in my hand. With all my strength I brought it up to the side of his head and hit him squarely in the temple. I hit him once and saw him go dizzy. I hit him again and saw him go down. Like a warrior, I suddenly had tremendous strength. I didn't know that I had it, but when someone is trying to attack you, kill you, you become powerful. You don't know how strong you can be until that moment. As he lay there I hit him again and saw the blood flowing out of his ear.

His friend who was driving the truck saw all this happening from inside the cab. He started yelling, "What the fuck is going on back there?" and looked for a place to pull the truck into the bushes. I knew it was over for me if he caught me. As the truck slowed down, I crawled to the back of the bed, and poised on the rocks, I jumped to the ground like a cat. Then I ran for my life.

The truck driver was an old man; he jumped out of the cab and screamed in a raspy voice, "You killed my friend! Come back! You killed him!" He chased me through the scrubby bushes for a short distance, then gave up. Or so I thought.

The driver went back, crawled inside his truck, fired it up, and started driving through the desert after me. The twin headlight beams illuminated the ground around me; I heard the roar of the truck behind me. I was running as fast as I could, but of course the truck was gaining on me. I zigzagged and circled back through the darkness. He couldn't keep me in sight, so finally he gave up and headed back to the road.

I ran through the desert like a hunted animal; I ran through desert, then jungle, then desert again, with no idea of where I was. The sun came up and I continued to run. Finally I came upon another road. Even though I was sick with fear at the thought of what might happen, I decided to hitchhike again, because I knew I needed to get as far away as possible from the truck driver and his friend. What happened to my attacker after I hit him with the stone, I've never known, but the last thing I wanted was to meet up with those two men again.

Standing on the side of the road in the morning sun, I must have been a pretty sight. The scarf I was wearing was now a filthy rag; I had been running through the sand for days and my skin and hair were coated with dust; my arms and legs looked like twigs that might snap in a hard wind and my feet were covered with sores that would rival a leper's. Holding my hand out, I flagged down a Mercedes. An elegantly dressed man pulled the car to the side of the road. I crawled onto the leather seat and gaped at the luxury of it. "Where are you going?" the man asked.

"That way," I said, and pointed straight ahead, in the direction the Mercedes was already traveling. The man opened his mouth, showing his beautiful white teeth, and started to laugh.

2.

GROWING UP
WITH ANIMALS

Before I ran away from home, my life had been built around nature, family, and our strong bond with the animals that kept us alive. Stretching back to my earliest days, I shared a common trait with children the world over: my love of animals. In fact, my earliest memory is of my pet goat, Billy. Billy was my special treasure, my everything, and maybe I loved him most because he was a baby, like me. I used to sneak him all the food I could find, until he was the plumpest, happiest little goat in the herd. My mother constantly questioned, "Why is this goat so fat, when all the rest are so skinny?" I took perfect care of him, grooming him, petting him, talking to him for hours.

My relationship with Billy was representative of our lives in Somalia. My family's fate intertwined with that of the herds we tended daily. Dependence on the animals created our great respect for them, and those feelings were present in everything we did. All the children in my family tended our animals, a task we began helping with as soon as we were able to walk.

We grew up with the animals, prospered when they prospered, suffered when they suffered, died when they died. We raised cattle, sheep, and goats, but while I dearly loved my little Billy, there was no doubt that our camels were the most important animals we owned.

The camel is legendary in Somalia; Somalia boasts more camels than any country in the world; there are more camels in Somalia than people. In my country we have a long tradition of oral poetry, and much of it is devoted to passing along the lessons of the camel from one generation to the next, telling of its essential value to our culture. I remember my mother used to sing us a song, which basically said, "My camel has gone away to the bad man, who will either kill it or steal it from me. So I'm begging, I'm praying, please bring back my camel." From the time I was a baby, I knew of the great importance of these animals, because they're absolutely gold in our society. You simply cannot live in the desert without them. As one Somali poet put it:

> *A she-camel is a mother*
> *To him who owns it*
> *Whereas a he-camel is the artery*
> *Onto which hangs life itself . . .*

And it's true. A man's life is measured by camels, with one hundred camels being the price for a man who has been killed. A hundred camels must be paid by the killer's clan to the surviving family of the victim, or the dead man's clan will attack the killer in retribution. The traditional price for a bride is paid in camels. But on a daily level, the camels kept us alive. No other domestic animal is so well suited for life in the desert. A camel wants to drink once a week, but can go as long as a month without water. In the meantime, however, the female camel gives milk to nourish us and quench our thirst, an enormous asset when you're far from water. Even in the hottest temperatures, camels retain liquid and survive. They graze on the scrubby bushes found in our arid landscape, leaving the grasses for the other livestock.

We raised them to carry us across the desert, haul our meager belongings, and pay our debts. In other countries, you might hop in your car and go, but our only transportation, other than walking, was our camels.

The animal's personality is very similar to that of a horse; a camel will develop a close relationship with his master, and do things for him that he wouldn't do for anybody else. Men break the young camels—a dangerous practice—and train them to be ridden and follow a lead. It's important to be firm with them, because otherwise, when they sense a weak rider, they'll buck him off, or kick him.

Like most Somalis, we lived the pastoral lifestyle of herdsmen. Even though we struggled constantly for survival, our large herds of camels, cattle, sheep, and goats marked us as wealthy by the standards in my country. Following tradition, my brothers usually tended the large animals, the cattle and camels, and the girls watched over the smaller ones.

As nomads we traveled constantly, never staying in one place for more than three or four weeks. This constant movement was driven by the need to care for our animals. We were seeking food and water to keep them alive, and in the dry Somalian climate these necessities were seldom easy to find.

Our home was a hut woven from grass; being portable, it served the same purpose as a tent. We built a framework from sticks, then my mother wove grass mats that we laid over the bent twigs to form a dome about six feet in diameter. When it came time to move on, we dismantled the hut and tied the sticks and mats, along with our few possessions, to the backs of our camels. They're incredibly strong animals, and the babies and small children would ride on top, while the rest of us walked alongside, herding the animals to our next home. When we found a spot with water and foliage for grazing, we'd set up our camp again.

———

The hut provided shelter for the babies, shade from the midday sun, and storage space for fresh milk. At night, the rest of us slept outside under the stars, with the children cuddled together on a mat. After the sun went down, the desert was cold; we didn't have enough blankets for each child to have his own, and since we had very little clothing, we used the heat from our bodies to keep us warm. My father slept off to one side, as our guardian, the protector of the family.

In the morning we got up with the sun. Our first chore was to head out to the pens where we kept the herds, and milk them. Wherever we went we cut saplings to make pens for the animals, to keep them from straying at night. The baby animals were kept in a pen separate from the mothers so they wouldn't take all the milk. One of my tasks was to milk the cows, taking some of the fresh milk to make butter, but leaving enough for the calves. After the milking, we'd let the babies come in and nurse.

Then we had our breakfast of camel's milk, which is more nutritious than other animals' milk as it contains vitamin C. Our region was very dry, without enough water to grow crops, so we had no vegetables or bread. Sometimes we followed warthogs, large wild African pigs, tracking them to plants. They sniffed out edible roots, digging down with their hooves and snouts to feast on them. Our family shared in their bounty by taking some home to add to our diet.

We looked at slaughtering animals for meat as wasteful, and only resorted to this in case of emergency, or for special occasions, such as a wedding. Our animals were too valuable for us to kill and eat, as we raised them for their milk and to trade for the other goods we needed. For everyday sustenance, we had only camel's milk for breakfast, and again in the evening for supper. Sometimes there wasn't enough for everybody, so we fed the smallest children first, then the older ones, and so on. My mother never took a bite of food until everyone else had eaten; in fact, I don't remember ever seeing my mother eat, although I realize she must have. But if we didn't have anything for supper at night, it was no big deal, nothing to panic about. No need to cry or complain. The little babies might cry, but the older children knew the rules, so we just went to sleep. We tried to remain cheerful, kept calm and quiet, and tomorrow, God willing, we'd find a way. *In'shallah*, which means it will happen "if God is willing," was our philosophy. We knew our lives were dependent on the forces of nature, and God controlled those forces, not us.

A big treat for us—as people in other parts of the world might regard a holiday feast—was when my father brought home a sack of rice. Then we'd use the butter we made by shaking cow's milk in a basket that my mother had woven. Occasionally we'd trade a goat for corn grown in the wetter regions of Somalia, and grind the corn into meal and make porridge, or pop it in a pan over the fire. Or, when other families were around, we always shared whatever we had. If one of us had some food—dates or roots—or maybe killed an animal for meat, we'd cook it and divide the meal among us. We shared our good fortune, because even though we were isolated most of the time, traveling with one or two other families, we were still part of a larger community. On the practical side, since there were no refrigerators, meat or anything fresh needed to be consumed right away.

Each morning after breakfast, it was time to take the animals from their pen. By the age of six, I was responsible for taking herds of about sixty or seventy sheep and goats into the desert to graze. I got my long stick and headed off alone with my herd, singing my little song to guide them. If one strayed from the group, I used my staff to guide it back. They were eager to go, because they realized coming out of the pen meant that it was time to eat. Getting an early head start was important, to find the best spot with fresh water and lots of grass. Each day I quickly searched for water, in order to beat the other herders; otherwise their animals would drink what little there was. In any case, as the sun grew hotter, the ground became so thirsty that it would suck it all up. I made sure the animals drank as much water as they could, because it might be another week before we found more. Or two. Or three—who knows? Sometimes during the drought the saddest thing was to watch all the animals die. We traveled further and further each day looking for water; the herd tried to make it, but eventually they couldn't go anymore. When they collapsed, you had the most helpless feeling in the world, because you knew that was the end and there was nothing you could do.

No one owns the grazing land in Somalia, so it was up to me to be cunning, and discover areas with lots of plants for my goats and sheep. My survival instincts were honed to look for signs of rain, and I scanned the sky for clouds. My other senses also came into play, because a particular smell or a certain feeling in the air predicted rain.

While the animals grazed, I watched for predators, which are everywhere in Africa. The hyenas would sneak up and snatch a lamb or kid that had wandered off from the herd. There were lions to worry about and wild dogs; they all traveled in packs, but there was only one of me.

Watching the sky, I carefully calculated how far I had to travel to return home before night fell. But many times I miscalculated, and that's when trouble began. As I was stumbling along in the dark, trying to get home, the hyenas would attack, because they knew I couldn't see them. I'd swat one here, and another would sneak up behind me. As I chased that one away, another would run up while I wasn't looking. The hyenas are the worst, because they're relentless; they never quit until they get something. When I got home each evening and put the animals in the pen, I counted several times to see if any were missing. One night I returned home with my herd, and as I counted my goats, I noticed I was one short. I counted again. And again. Suddenly I realized I hadn't seen Billy, and hurried through the goats checking for him. I ran to my mother screaming, "Mama, Billy's missing—what should I do?" But of course it was too late, so she simply stroked my head as I cried when I realized that the hyenas had eaten my fat little pet.

Whatever else happened to us, the responsibility of taking care of our livestock went on and was always our first priority, even in times of drought, sickness, or war. Somalia's constant political turmoil caused enormous problems in the cities, but we were so isolated that for the most part no one bothered us. Then, when I was about nine years old, a large army came and camped close by. We'd heard stories about soldiers raping girls they caught out alone, and I knew a girl this had happened to. It didn't matter if they were the Somalian army or the Martian army, they were not part of our people; they were not nomads, and we avoided them at all costs.

One morning my father had given me the chore of watering the camels, so I headed off with the herd. Evidently, during the night, the army had arrived, and now sat encamped all around the road, their tents and trucks stretching as far as I could see. I hid behind a tree and watched them milling about in their uniforms. I was frightened, remembering the other girl's story; certainly I had no one around to protect me, so the men were free to do whatever they pleased. At first sight I hated them. I hated their uniforms, I hated their trucks, I hated their guns. I didn't even know what they were doing; for all I knew they could have been saving Somalia, but I didn't want any part of them all the same. Yet my camels needed water. The only route I knew that would avoid the army camp was too long and circuitous for me to travel with my herd, so I decided to turn the camels loose, and let them walk through the camp without me. They marched right through the middle of the soldiers, making straight for the water, as I had hoped they would. I scurried around the camp, ducking behind bushes and trees, until I joined the camels on the other side at the watering hole.

Then, as the sky grew dark, we repeated the procedure and headed home safely.

Each evening, when I returned home at sunset and secured my herd back in the pen, it was time to start the milking again. Around the camels' necks we hung wooden bells. The sound of these bells is indeed music to the nomad, who listens to their hollow clunk at twilight as the milking begins. The bells always act as a beacon to the traveler searching for home as the light fades. During the ritual of our evening chores, the great curve of the desert sky darkens, and a bright planet appears, a signal that it's time to herd the sheep into their pen. In other nations this planet is known as Venus, the planet of love, but in my country we call it *maqal hidhid*, meaning "hiding the lambs."

Frequently, it was around this time I would get into trouble, because after working since sunup, I couldn't hold my eyes open any longer. Walking through the dusk, I'd fall asleep and the goats would bump into me, or as I squatted milking, my head would begin to nod. If my father caught me dozing off, watch out! I love my father, but he could be a son of a gun; when he caught me sleeping on the job he'd beat me, to make sure I took my work seriously and paid attention to my business. After we finished our chores, we'd have our supper of camel's milk. Then we'd gather wood for a big fire and sit around its warmth talking and laughing until we went to sleep.

Those evenings are my favorite memories of Somalia: sitting around with my mother and father, sisters and brothers, when everybody was full, everybody was laughing. We always tried to be upbeat, optimistic. Nobody sat around complaining or whining or saying, "Hey, let's have a conversation about death." Life there was very hard; we needed all our strength just to survive and being negative sapped our vital energy.

Even though we were far from any village, I was never lonely, because I played with my sisters and brothers. I was a middle child, with an older brother and two older sisters and several younger siblings. We chased each other endlessly, climbed trees like monkeys, played tic-tac-toe in the sand by drawing lines with our fingers, collected pebbles, and dug holes in the ground to play an African game called mancala. We even had our own version of jacks, but instead of a rubber ball and metal pieces, we threw up one rock and grabbed other rocks in place of the jacks. This was my favorite because I was very good at it, and I always tried to get my little brother, Ali, to play it with me.

Our greatest pleasure, though, was pure joy at being a child in the wilderness, the freedom to be part of nature and experience its sights, sounds, and smells. We watched packs of lions lie around all day, baking in the sun, rolling onto their backs, sticking their feet up in the air and snoring. The cubs chased each other and played just as we did. We ran with the giraffes, the zebras, the foxes. The hyrax, an African animal that's the size of a rabbit but is actually a descendant of the elephant, was a particular favorite. We waited patiently outside their burrows for their little faces to appear, then chased them through the sand.

Once, on an excursion, I discovered an ostrich egg. I decided to take it home with me because I wanted to watch the baby ostrich hatch, then keep it as a pet. The egg is about the size of a bowling ball, and I hoisted it up from its hole in the sand and was carrying it away when Mama Ostrich came after me. She chased me—and believe me, ostriches are fast; they can run forty miles an hour. She quickly caught me and started pecking my head with her beak, ka-ka-ka. I thought she was going to crack my skull like an egg, so I put down her baby and ran for my life.

Seldom were we close to forested areas, but when we were, we loved to see the elephants. From a great distance we'd hear their thundering roar and climb a tree to spot them. Like lions, monkeys, and humans, elephants live in communities. If they had a baby in their midst, every adult elephant, the cousin, the uncle, the auntie, the sister, the mother, the grand—all of them would watch after that baby, to make sure nobody touched it. All of us children would stand high in the top of a tree and laugh, watching the elephant world for hours.

But gradually all those happy times with my family disappeared. My sister ran away; my brother went to school in the city. I learned sad facts about our family, about life. The rain stopped coming, and taking care of our animals was more and more difficult. Life became harder. And I became harder with it.

Part of that hardness formed watching my brothers and sisters die. Originally there were twelve children in my family, but now there are only six of us left. My mother had a set of twins who died right after they were born. She had another beautiful baby girl who was about six months old. One day the baby was strong and healthy, the next my mother called to me, "Waris!!!" I ran to her and saw her kneeling over the baby. I was just a little girl, but I could tell something was terribly wrong, the baby didn't look right. "Waris, run get me some camel's milk!" my mother commanded. But I couldn't move. "Run, hurry!" I stood staring at my sister in a trance—in terror. "What's wrong with you?" Mama screamed at me.

Finally, I tore myself away, but I knew what would be waiting for me when I got back. I returned with the milk, but the baby was totally still, and I knew she was dead. When I looked at my sister again, Mama slapped me hard. For a long time she blamed me for the baby's death, feeling that I had some sort of sorcerer's powers, and when in my trance I stared at the baby, I caused its death.

I had no such powers, but my little brother did have supernatural gifts. Everyone agreed he was no ordinary child. We called him Old Man, because when he was roughly six, his hair turned completely gray. He was extremely intelligent, and every man around us came to ask for his advice. They would walk up and say: "Where's the Old Man?" Then, by turns, they would sit this little gray-haired boy on their laps. "What do you think about the rain this year?" they would ask. And honest to God, even though in years he was a child, never did he act like a child. He thought, talked, sat, and behaved like a very wise elderly man. While everyone respected him, they were frightened of him, too, because he was so obviously not one of us. While he was still technically a young boy, Old Man died, as if in a few short years he'd crammed in an entire lifetime. No one knew the cause, but everyone felt his passing made sense, because: "There's no way he belonged to this world."

As in any large family, each of us developed a role. Mine became the role of rebel, a reputation I earned in a series of actions that to me seemed perfectly logical and justified, but to my elders— particularly my father—seemed outrageous. One day my younger brother, Ali, and I sat under a tree eating white rice with camel's milk. Ali wolfed his down greedily, but because this was a rare treat for us, I took each bite slowly. Having food was not something we took for granted; I always appreciated mine, savoring each bite with pleasure. Only a small amount of rice and milk remained in my bowl, and I anticipated it eagerly. Suddenly Ali stuck his spoon in my dish and scooped out my last bite, taking every last grain of rice. Without thinking, I retaliated by grabbing up a knife lying next to me and burying the blade in Ali's thigh. He shrieked, but took it out and sunk the knife in exactly the same spot in my leg. Now both of us sat with wounded legs, but because I was the one who had struck first, the blame went to me. Today, we carry matching scars from this meal.

One of the earliest outbursts of my rebel behavior centered on my longing for a pair of shoes. All my life I've been obsessed by shoes. Today even though I'm a model, I don't own many clothes—a pair of jeans, a couple of T-shirts—but I have a cupboard stacked full of high heels, sandals, tennis shoes, loafers, and boots, even though ironically I have nothing to wear them with. As a child I desperately wanted shoes, but not all the children in my family had clothes, and certainly there was no money to buy shoes. Yet it was my dream to wear beautiful leather sandals like my mother wore. How I wished to put on a pair of comfortable shoes and look after my animals, walk without worrying about rocks and thorns, snakes and scorpions. My feet were always bruised and marked, and I still carry the black scars today. Once a thorn came all the way through my foot; sometimes they would break off in my feet. We had no doctors in the desert, or medicine to treat the wound. But still we had to walk, because we had to look after the animals. No one said, "I can't." We just did it, went out each morning and limped along as best we could.

One of my father's brothers was a very wealthy man. Uncle Ahmed lived in the city, in Galcaio, but we looked after his camels and the rest of his animals. I was the favorite to care for his goats, because I always did a thorough job, making sure they were well fed and watered, and I did my best to keep them safe from predators. One day, when I was about seven years old, Uncle Ahmed visited us and I said, "Look, I want you to buy me some shoes."

He looked at me and laughed. "Yeah, yeah, all right. I'll get you shoes." I knew he was surprised, because it was very unusual for a girl to ask for anything, let alone anything as extravagant as shoes.

The next time my father took me to see him, I was excited, because today would be the day I got my first pair of shoes. At my earliest opportunity I said eagerly, "Well, did you bring them?"

He said, "Yeah, I have them right here," and handed me a parcel. I took the shoes in my hand and examined them; they were rubber sandals, flip-flops. Not beautiful leather sandals like Mama's, but cheap, yellow flip-flops. I couldn't believe it.

"*These are my shoes?!*" I cried, and threw them at him. When the flip-flops bounced off his brother's face, my father tried to be upset, but this time he couldn't help himself—he doubled over laughing.

My uncle said to him, "I don't believe it. How are you raising this child?"

I started fighting with my uncle, swinging at him, because I was so disappointed, I was furious. "I worked so hard for this shit!" I screamed. "I did all this work for you, and this is it? I get a pair of cheap rubber sandals? Fah!! I'd rather go barefoot— I'll go barefoot till my feet bleed before I wear this garbage!" and I motioned toward his gift.

Uncle Ahmed just looked at me, then raised his eyes to heaven and moaned, "Oh, Allah." He stooped with a sigh, picked up his flip-flops, and took them back home.

I was not content to give up so easily, however. After that day I kept sending my uncle messages by every relative, friend, or stranger heading to Galcaio: "Waris wants shoes!" But I had to wait many years until I realized my dream of owning a pair. In the meantime, however, I continued to raise Uncle Ahmed's goats, and help my family care for our herds, walking thousands of miles barefoot.

Several years before the shoes episode with Uncle Ahmed, when I was a tiny girl, around four years old, we had a visitor one day. The man, Guban, was a good friend of my father's and frequently came to see us. At twilight he stood talking with my parents, until finally my mother, staring at the sky, watching the bright planet *maqal hidhid* emerge, said it was time to bring in the lambs. Guban said, "Oh, why don't you let me do that for you? Waris can help me."

I felt important at being chosen over the boys to help Papa's friend with the animals. He took my hand and we walked away from the hut and began to round up the herd. Normally I would have been running everywhere like a wild animal myself, but it was getting dark now, and since I was frightened, I stayed close to Guban. Suddenly he took off his jacket and laid it on the sand and sat down on top of it. I stared at him, confused, and protested: "Why are you sitting down? It's getting dark—we have to get the animals."

"We have time. We'll do that in a minute." He rested on one side of his jacket and patted the empty space next to him. "Come sit down."

Reluctantly I came to him. Since I always loved stories as a kid, I realized this might be a good opportunity to hear one. "Will you tell me a story?"

Guban patted his coat again. "If you sit down, I'll tell you one." As soon as I sat next to him, he started trying to push me back onto his coat. "I don't want to lie down. I want you to tell me a story," I insisted stubbornly and squirmed upright.

"Come, come." His hand pushed my shoulder firmly. "Lie down and look at the stars and I'll tell you a story." Stretching out with my head on his jacket, I stuck my toes in the cold sand and stared at the phosphorescent Milky Way. As the sky deepened from indigo to black, the lambs ran in circles around us, crying in the dark, and I waited anxiously for the story to begin. Abruptly, Guban's face came between me and the Milky Way; he squatted between my legs and yanked up the little scarf wrapped around my waist. Next I felt something hard and wet pressing against my vagina. I froze at first, not understanding what was happening, but I knew it was something very bad. The pressure intensified until it became a sharp pain.

"I want my Mama!" Suddenly I was flooded with a warm liquid and a sickening acrid odor permeated the night air. "You pee-peed on me!" I screamed, horrified. I jumped up and rubbed my scarf against my legs, mopping off the foul-smelling liquid.

"No, no, it's okay," he whispered soothingly and grabbed my arm. "I was just trying to tell you a story." Jerking free, I ran back to my mother, with Guban chasing after me, trying to catch me. When I saw Mama standing next to the fire, the orange light glowing off her face, I ran up and threw my arms around her legs.

"What's wrong, Waris?" Mama said in alarm. Guban ran up behind me panting, and my mother looked at him. "What happened to her?"

He laughed casually and waved his arm at me. "Oh, I was trying to tell her a story and she got scared." I held on to my mother with a grip of iron. I wanted to tell her what Papa's friend had done to me, but I didn't have the words—I didn't *know* what he'd done. I looked at his smiling face in the firelight, a face I would have to see again and again over the years, and knew I'd hate him forever.

She stroked my head as I pressed my face into her thigh. "Waris, it's okay. There, there, it was only a story, baby. It's not *real*." To Guban, she said, "Where are the lambs?"

3.

A NOMAD'S LIFE

Growing up in Africa I did not have the sense of history that seems so important in other parts of the world. Our language, Somali, did not have a written script until 1973, so we did not learn to read or write. Knowledge was passed down by word of mouth—poetry or folktales—or, more important, by our parents teaching us the skills we needed to survive. For example, my mother taught me how to weave from dried grass containers tight enough to hold milk; my father taught me how to care for our animals and make sure they were healthy. We didn't spend much time talking about the past—nobody had time for that. Everything was today, what are we going to do *today*? Are all the children in? Are all the animals safe? How are we going to eat? Where can we find water?

In Somalia, we lived the way our ancestors had for thousands of years; nothing had changed dramatically for us. As nomads we did not live with electricity, telephones, or automobiles, much less computers, television, or space travel. These facts, combined with our emphasis on living in the present, gave us a much different perspective on time than the one that dominates the Western world.

Like the rest of my family, I have no idea how old I am; I can only guess. A baby who is born in my country has little guarantee of being alive one year later, so the concept of tracking birthdays does not retain the same importance. When I was a child, we lived without artificial time constructions of schedules, clocks, and calendars. Instead, we lived by the seasons and the sun, planning our moves around our need for rain, planning our day around the span of daylight available. We told time by using the sun. If my shadow was on the west side, it was morning; when it moved directly underneath me, it was noon. When my shadow crossed to the other side, it was afternoon. As the day grew longer, so did my shadow—my cue to start heading home before dark.

When we got up in the morning, we decided what we'd do that day, then did that task the best we could until we finished or the sky grew too dark for us to see. There was no such notion of getting up and having your day all planned out for you. In New York, people frequently whip out their datebooks and ask, "Are you free for lunch on the fourteenth—or what about the fifteenth?" I respond with "Why don't you call me the day before you want to meet up?" No matter how many times I write down appointments, I can't get used to the idea. When I first came to London, I was mystified by the connection between people staring at their wrist, then crying, "I've got to dash!" I felt like everyone was rushing everywhere, every action was timed. In Africa there was no hurry, no stress. African time is very, very slow, very calm. If you say, "I'll see you tomorrow around noon," that means about four or five o'clock. And today I still refuse to wear a watch.

During my childhood years in Somalia, it never occurred to me to fast-forward into the future, or delve into the past enough to ask, "Mama, how did you grow up?" As a consequence I know little of my family history, especially since I left home at such an early age. I constantly wish I could go back and ask those questions now—ask my mother what her life was like when she was a little girl, or ask where her mother came from, or how her father died. It disturbs me that I may never know these facts.

However, one thing I do know about my mother is that she was very beautiful. I know I sound like the typical adoring daughter, but she was. Her face was like a Modigliani sculpture, and her skin so dark and smooth, that she looked as if she'd been perfectly chiseled from black marble. Since Mama's skin was jet black and her teeth dazzlingly white, at night when she smiled all you could see were her teeth glowing, as if they floated all by themselves in the night. Her hair was long and straight, very soft, and she'd smooth it with her fingers, since she never owned a comb. My mother is tall and slender—traits that all her daughters inherited.

Her demeanor is very calm, very quiet. But when she starts talking, she's hysterically funny and she laughs a lot. She tells jokes, and some of them are funny, some are really dirty, and some are just stupid little things she'd say to crack us up. She'd look at me and say, "Waris, why are your eyes disappearing into your face?" But her favorite silly joke was calling me Avdohol, which means "small mouth." Mama would look at me for no reason and say, "Hey, Avdohol, why is your mouth so small?"

My father was very handsome, and believe me, he knew it. He was about six feet tall, slim, and lighter than Mama; his hair was brown, and his eyes were light brown. Papa was cocky because he knew he was good-looking. He always teased Mama, "I can go and get another woman if you don't—" and then he'd fill in the blank with whatever he was after. Or, "Look, I'm getting bored around here. I'm getting me another woman. . . ." My mother would tease back, "Go ahead. See what you can do." They really loved each other, but unfortunately one day these taunts came true.

My mother grew up in Mogadishu, the capital city of Somalia. My father, on the other hand, was a nomad and had always lived roaming the desert. When she met him, my mother thought Papa was so handsome that a life wandering with him as nomads sounded like a romantic idea; they quickly decided to get married. Papa went to my grandmother, since my grandfather was dead, and asked permission to marry my mother. My grandmother said, "No, no, *no*, absolutely not." To my mother she added, "He's just a playboy!" Grandmother was not about to allow her beautiful daughter to throw her life away raising camels in the wilderness with *this man*, this desert man! However, when my mother was about sixteen, she ran away and married Papa anyhow.

They went to the other side of the country and lived with his family in the desert, which created a whole series of problems for my mother. Her family had money and power, and she had never known this type of harsh nomadic life. Greater than that dilemma, however, was the fact that my father was from the Daarood tribe, and my mother was from the Hawiye tribe. Like Native Americans, the citizens of Somalia are divided into individual tribes, and each has a fanatical loyalty to its own group. This tribal pride has been the source of wars throughout our history.

A great rivalry exists between the Daaroods and Hawiyes, and my father's family always treated my mother badly, assuming she was a lesser mortal by virtue of being from a different tribe than their own. Mama was lonely for a very long time, but she had to adapt. After I ran away from home and was separated from my family, I realized what life must have been like for her, living all alone among the Daaroods.

My mother started having babies, and raising her children gave her the love she missed being away from her own people. But again, now that I'm grown, I look back and realize what she went through having twelve children. I remember when Mama was pregnant, she would suddenly disappear, and we wouldn't see her for days. Then she would show up—carrying a tiny baby. She went off into the desert alone and gave birth, taking along something sharp to cut the umbilical cord. Once after she disappeared we had to move our camp in the endless search for water. It took her four days to find us; she walked across the desert carrying the newborn baby while she looked for her husband.

Of all her children, though, I always felt I was my mother's special favorite. We had a strong bond of understanding between us, and I still think about her every day of my life, praying to God to take care of her until I'm able to do the job. As a child I always wanted to be near her, and all day I would look forward to coming home in the evening when I would sit next to Mama and she would stroke my head.

My mother wove beautiful baskets, a skill that takes years of practice to achieve. We spent many hours together as she taught me how to make a small cup that I could drink milk from, but my attempts at larger projects were never like hers. My baskets were raggedy and full of holes.

One day my desire to be with Mama and my natural childish curiosity drove me to secretly follow her. Once a month she left our camp and went away by herself for the afternoon. I said to her, "I'm so determined to know what you do, Mom—what is this thing you do every month?" She told me to mind my own business; a child in Africa has no right meddling in parents' affairs. And, as usual, she told me to stay home and watch after the younger children. But when she walked away, I hurried behind her at a distance, hiding behind bushes to stay out of sight. She met with five other women, who had traveled long distances also. Together they sat under a huge, beautiful tree for several hours during our siesta, when the sun was too hot to do much else. During that time the animals and family were all resting, so they could spare a little time for themselves. Their black heads gathered close in the distance like ants, and I watched as they ate popcorn and drank tea. What they talked about, I still don't know, as I was too far away to hear. Eventually I decided to risk revealing myself, mainly because I wanted some of their food. I walked up meekly and stood next to my mother.

"Where did you come from?" she cried.

"I followed you."

"Bad, naughty girl," she scolded.

But all the other women laughed, and cooed, "Oh, look at the cute little girl. Come here, darling . . ." So my mother relented and let me have some popcorn.

When I was this young age, I had no conception of another world different from the one we lived in with our goats and camels. Without travel to different countries, books, TV, or movies, my universe simply consisted of the sights I saw around me each day. I certainly had no conception that my mother had come from a different life. Before Somalia's independence in 1960, Italy had colonized the southern region. As a result, Mogadishu's culture, architecture, and society were full of Italian influences, so my mother spoke Italian. Occasionally, when she was angry, she'd spew a string of Italian cusswords. "Mama!" I'd look at her in alarm. "What are you saying?"

"Oh, that's Italian."

"What's Italian? What does it mean?"

"Nothing—mind your own business," and she'd wave me aside.

Later I discovered for myself—like I discovered cars and buildings—that Italian was part of a broader world outside our hut. Many times we children questioned Mama about her decision to marry our father. "Why did you ever follow this man? Look where you're living, while your brothers and sisters are living all over the world—they're ambassadors and what have you! Why did you run away with this loser?" She replied that she'd fallen in love with Papa, and made her decision to run away with him so they could be together. Yet my mother is a strong, strong woman. In spite of everything I watched her go through, I never heard her complain. I never heard her say, "I'm fed up with this," or "I'm not doing this anymore." Mama was simply silent and hard as iron. Then without warning, she'd crack us up with one of her silly jokes. My goal is to someday be as strong as she is, then I can say my life has been a success.

Our family was typical in our choice of occupations, since over 60 percent of Somalis are pastoral nomads, earning a living by raising animals. My father periodically ventured into a village and sold an animal in order to buy a sack of rice, fabric for clothes, or blankets. Occasionally, he sent along his goods for sale with anybody traveling into town, and a shopping list of items he wanted purchased in return.

Another way we made money was by harvesting frankincense, the incense mentioned in the Bible as one of the gifts the Magi brought the baby Jesus. Its scent is still a valued commodity today, as it has been since ancient times. Frankincense comes from the Boswellia tree, which grows in the highlands of northeastern Somalia. It's a beautiful little tree, about five feet tall, and the limbs hang in a curve like an open umbrella. I would take an ax and strike the tree lightly—not enough to damage it—just enough to slash the bark. Then the tree would bleed a milky fluid. I waited a day for the white juice to harden into gum; in fact, sometimes we would chew it like gum for its bitter taste. We gathered the clumps into baskets, then my father sold them. My family also burned frankincense at night in our campfires, and whenever I smell it today I'm transported back to those evenings. Sometimes, in Manhattan, I'll find incense advertised as frankincense. Desperate for a little reminder of home, I buy it, but its smell is such a weak imitation that it can never match the rich exotic perfume of our fires burning in the desert night.

Our large family was also typical in Somalia, where the average woman has seven children. Children are looked at as the future old-age pension for the elders, as they will take care of their parents when they grow old. Somali children regard their parents and grandparents with great respect, never daring to question their authority. All your elders, even your older brothers and sisters, must be treated with respect, and you must follow their wishes. This fact was one of the reasons my rebellious acts were considered so incredibly scandalous.

Part of the reason for large families, other than lack of birth control, is that the more people who share the work, the easier life is. Even basic functions such as having water—not plenty of water, or enough water, but any water at all—required back-breaking work. When the area around us dried up, my father went in search of water. He strapped huge bags onto our camels, bags my mother had woven from grass. Then he left home and was gone for days until he found water, filled the bags, and traveled back to us. We tried to stay in one spot waiting for him, but each day would become increasingly challenging, as we traveled miles and miles to water the herds. Sometimes we had to move on without him, yet he always found us, even without the aid of roads, street signs, or maps. Or, if my father was away, if he'd gone to the village in search of food, one of the children had to do this job, because Mama had to stay home and keep everything running.

Sometimes the job fell to me. I'd walk and walk for days, however long it took to find water, because there was no point in coming back without it. We knew never to come home empty- handed, because then there was no hope. We had to keep going until we found something. No one accepted the excuse "I can't." My mother told me to find water, so I had to find water. When I came to the Western world, I was amazed to find people complaining, "I can't work because I have a headache." I wanted to say to them, "Let me give you hard work. You'll never complain about your job again."

One of the techniques for providing more hands to ease the workload was increasing the number of women and children, which means that having multiple wives is a common practice in Africa. My parents were unusual in that only the two of them were together as a couple for years and years. Finally, one day, after having twelve children, my mother said, "I'm too old . . . why don't you get yourself another wife and give me a break? Leave me alone now." I don't know if she meant it or not—she probably never thought my father would take her up on it.

But one day, Papa disappeared. At first we thought he'd gone in search of water, or food, and my mother looked after everything by herself. After he'd been gone for two months, we thought he was dead. Then one evening, as suddenly as he'd left, my father reappeared. All the children were sitting around in front of our hut. He strolled up and said, "Where's your mother?" We told him she was still out with the animals. "Well, hey-hey, everyone," he said, grinning, "I want you to meet my wife." He pulled forward this little girl, about seventeen years old—not much older than I was. We all just stared at her, because we weren't allowed to say anything; besides, we didn't know *what* to say.

When my mother came home, it was a horrible moment. All the children waited tensely to see what would happen. Mama glared at my father, not noticing the other woman in the darkness, and said, "Oh, you decided to show up, did you?"

Papa shifted his weight from one foot to the other, and looked around. "Yeah, well, yeah. By the way, meet my wife," and he put his arm around his new bride. I can never forget my mother's face in the firelight. It just fell to the ground. Then she realized, "Damn, I lost him now to this little, little girl!" Mama was dying from jealousy, although, bless her heart, she tried so hard not to show it.

We had no idea where my father's new wife was from, nor did

we know anything about her. But that didn't stop her from immediately bossing all his children around. Next this seventeen-year-old girl started bossing my mother around— telling Mama to do this, get me that, cook me this. Things were already growing very tense when one day she made a fatal mistake: she slapped my brother Old Man.

The day this happened all we kids were in our hangout (each time we moved, we found a tree close to the hut that was the children's "room"). One day I was sitting under this tree with my brothers and sisters when I heard Old Man crying. I stood up and spotted my little brother walking toward me. "What's wrong with you? What happened?" I said, bending over to wipe his face.

"She slapped me—she slapped me so hard." I didn't even have to ask who, because no one in our family had ever hit Old Man. Not my mother, not any of his older siblings, not even my father, who beat the rest of us on a regular basis. There was no need to hit Old Man, since he was the wisest one among us and always did the right thing. Slapping my brother was the breaking point; this was more than I could stand, and I went looking for this foolish girl.

"Why did you slap my brother?" I demanded.

"He drank my milk," she said in her haughty way, as if she were the queen and owned all our milk from our herds.

"*Your* milk? I put that milk in the hut, and if he wants it, if he's thirsty, he can have it. You don't need to hit him!"

"Oh, shut the hell up and get away from me!" she yelled, dismissing me with a wave of her hand. I stared at her and shook my head, because even though I was only about thirteen, I knew she'd made a big mistake.

My brothers and sisters sat waiting under the tree, straining to hear the conversation between Papa's wife and me. As I approached them, I pointed at their questioning faces and said, "Tomorrow." They nodded.

The next day luck was with us, because my father said he was leaving for a couple of days. When it was time for siesta I brought my animals home and found my sister and two brothers. "Papa's new little wife is taking over," I began, stating the obvious. "We've got to do something to teach her a lesson, because this has to stop."

"Yeah, but what are we going to do?" asked Ali.

"You'll see. Just come with me, and help me out." I got a thick, tough rope, the rope we used to tie our belongings onto the camels when we were traveling. We led Papa's scared wife away from our camp, took her into the bushes, and forced her to take off all her clothes. Then I threw one end of the rope around the limb of a huge tree and tied it around Little Wife's ankles. She alternated between cussing us, screaming, and sobbing while we pulled the rope and hauled her up off the ground. My brothers and I played the rope back and forth to position her head dangling about eight feet from the dirt, ensuring no wild animals could eat her. Then we tied the rope off and returned home, leaving her there—twisting and screaming in the desert.

The next afternoon, my father showed up a day early. He asked us where his little woman was. We all shrugged and said we hadn't seen her. Fortunately, we'd taken her far enough away so no one could hear her screaming. "Hmmm," he said, and looked at us suspiciously. By dark he still hadn't found any trace of her. Papa knew something was very, very wrong, and began questioning us: "When did you see her last? Have you seen her today? Did you see her yesterday?" We told him she hadn't come home the night before, which was, of course, true.

My father panicked and began frantically searching for her everywhere. But he didn't find her until the next morning. Father's bride had been hanging upside down for nearly two days by the time he cut her down, and she was in bad shape. By the time he came home he was furious. "Who's responsible for this?" he demanded. We all went quiet and looked at each other. Of course she told him. She said, "Waris was the leader. She attacked me first!" Papa came after me and started beating me, but all the kids jumped on him. We knew it was wrong to hit our own father, but we simply couldn't take it anymore.

After that day, Papa's new little wife was a changed person. We had set out to teach her a lesson, and she learned it well. After having the blood rush to her head for two days, I guess her brain was refreshed and she turned sweet and polite. From that point on, she kissed my mother's feet and waited on her like a slave. "What can I get you? What can I do for you? No, no—I'll do that. You sit down and relax."

And I thought, "There you go. You should have acted like this from the beginning, you little bitch, and saved us all that unnecessary grief." But the nomad's life is a harsh one, and even though she was twenty years younger than my mother, father's new wife wasn't as strong. In the end Mama learned she had nothing to fear from this little girl.

The nomad's life is a harsh one, but it is also full of beauty—a life so connected to nature that the two are inseparable. My mother named me after a miracle of nature: Waris means desert flower. The desert flower blooms in a barren environment where few living things can survive. Sometimes it doesn't rain in my country for over a year. But finally the water pours down, cleansing the dusty landscape, and then like a miracle the blooms appear. The flowers are a brilliant yellowish orange, and for this reason, yellow has always been my favorite color.

When a girl marries, the women from her tribe go out into the desert and collect these flowers. They dry them, then add water to them and make a paste to spread on the bride's face that gives her a golden glow. They decorate her hands and feet with henna, drawing ornate designs. They rim her eyes with kohl, so they look deep and sexy. All these cosmetics are made from plants and herbs, so they're completely natural. Next the women drape her in brightly colored scarves—reds and pinks and oranges and yellows—the more the better. Maybe they don't own much; many families are incredibly poor, but there is no shame over this fact. She'll simply wear the best she or her mother or sisters or friends can find, and carry herself with fierce pride—a trait all Somalis bear. By the time her wedding day comes, she walks out to greet her groom as a stunning beauty. The man doesn't deserve it!

For their wedding, the people in the tribe bring gifts; again, there's no need to feel pressured to buy certain things, or worry that you can't afford something better. You give whatever you have: weave a mat for them to sleep on, or give them a bowl, or if you have none of these, bring some food for the celebration after the ceremony. There's no such thing in my culture as a honeymoon, so the day after the wedding is a workday for the newlyweds, and they will need all their gifts to start their married life together.

Other than weddings, we have few celebrations. There are no holidays arbitrarily marked by a calendar. Instead, the other major cause for rejoicing is the long-awaited rain. In my country water is so scarce, yet it is the very essence of life. Nomads living in the desert have a deep, deep respect for water, regarding every drop as a precious commodity, and to this day I love water. Simply looking at it gives me great joy.

After months and months of drought, sometimes we would grow desperate. When this happened, the people would gather together and pray to God for rain. Sometimes it worked and sometimes it didn't. One year we had passed into what was supposed to be the rainy season, but still not a drop had fallen. Half our animals were dead and the other half were weak from thirst. My mother told me that we were all going to gather to pray for rain. The people converged, seemingly from out of nowhere. We were all praying and singing and dancing, trying to be happy and lift our spirits.

The next morning the clouds gathered, and the rain began to pour. Then, as always when it rains, the true rejoicing began. We would strip off our clothes and run into the water, splashing, and washing for the first time in months. The people celebrate with our traditional dancing: the women clapping their hands and chanting, their low sweet voices humming across the desert night, and the men leaping high into the air. Everyone contributes food, and we eat like kings to praise the gift of life.

In the days after the rains, the savannahs blossom with golden flowers, and the grasslands turn green. The animals are able to eat and drink their fill, offering us a chance to relax and enjoy life. We can go to the lakes newly created by the rain and bathe and swim. In the fresh air, the birds begin to sing and the nomads' desert becomes paradise.

4.

BECOMING A
WOMAN

The time had come for my oldest sister, Aman, to be circumcised. Like all younger siblings, I was envious, jealous that she was entering this grown-up world that was still closed to me. Aman was a teenager, much older than the normal age for circumcision, but so far the timing had never been right. As my family traveled Africa in our endless cycle, we had somehow missed the gypsy woman who performed this ancient ritual. When my father finally found her, he brought her to circumcise my two oldest sisters, Aman and Halemo. But when the woman came to our camp, Aman happened to be off searching for water, so the gypsy circumcised only Halemo. My father was growing concerned, because Aman was reaching marriageable age, but no marriage could take place unless she had been properly "fixed." The prevailing wisdom in Somalia is that there are bad things between a girl's legs, parts of our bodies that we're born with, yet are unclean. These things need to be removed—the clitoris, labia minora, and most of the labia majora are cut off, then the wound is stitched shut, leaving only a scar where our genitals had been. But the actual details of the ritual cutting are left a mystery—it's never explained to the girls. You just know that something special is going to happen to you when your time comes.

As a result, all young girls in Somalia anxiously await the ceremony that will mark their transformation from being a little girl to becoming a woman. Originally the process occurred when the girls reached puberty, and the ritual had some meaning, as the girl became fertile and capable of bearing her own children. But through time, female circumcision has been performed on younger and younger girls, partially due to pressure from the girls themselves, since they eagerly await their "special time" as a child in the West might await her birthday party, or Santa Claus's arrival on Christmas Eve.

When I heard the old gypsy was coming to circumcise Aman, I wanted to be circumcised, too. Aman was my beautiful older sister, my idol, and anything she wanted or had, I wanted, too. The day before the big event, I begged my mother, tugging at her arm, "Mama, do both of us at the same time. Come on, Mama, do both of us tomorrow!"

Mother pushed me away. "Just hush, little girl." However, Aman was not so eager. I remember her muttering, "I just hope I don't wind up like Halemo." But at the time I was too young to know what that meant, and when I asked Aman to explain she just changed the subject.

Very early the next morning my mother and her friend took Aman to meet the woman who would perform the circumcision. As usual, I pleaded to go, too, but Mama told me to stay home with the younger children. But using the same sneaky techniques I used the day I followed my mother to meet her friends, I followed along, hiding behind bushes and trees, staying a safe distance behind the group of women.

The gypsy woman arrived. She is considered an important person in our community, not only because she has specialized knowledge, but because she earns a great deal of money from

---

41

performing circumcisions. Paying for this procedure is one of the greatest expenses a household will undergo, but is still considered a good investment, since without it, the daughters will not make it onto the marriage market. With their genitals intact, they are considered unfit for marriage, unclean sluts whom no man would consider taking as a wife. So the gypsy woman, as some call her, is an important member of our society, but I call her the Killer Woman because of all the little girls who have died at her hand.

Peering from behind a tree, I watched my sister sit on the ground. Then my mother and her friend both grabbed Aman's shoulders and held her down. The gypsy started doing something between my sister's legs, and I saw a look of pain flash across Aman's face. My sister was a big girl, and very powerful, and suddenly—*phoom!* She raised her foot and shoved against the gypsy's chest, knocking her over on her back. Then my sister struggled free from the women holding her down, and leaped to her feet. To my horror, I saw blood pouring down her legs and onto the sand, leaving a trail as she ran. They all ran after her, but Aman was far ahead of them until she collapsed and fell to the ground. The women rolled her over on the spot where she had fallen, and continued their work. I felt sick and couldn't watch anymore, so I ran home.

Now I knew something I really wished I didn't know. I didn't understand what had happened, but was terrified at the thought of going through it myself. I couldn't very well ask my mother about it, because I wasn't supposed to have witnessed it. They kept Aman separated from the rest of the children while she healed, and two days later I took her some water. I knelt beside her and asked quietly, "What was it like?"

"Oh, it was horrible . . ." she began. But I guess she thought better of telling me the truth, knowing that I would have to be circumcised, and then I'd be frightened, instead of looking forward to it. "Anyway, you're not far from it; they will do it to you soon enough." And that's all she would say.

From then on, I dreaded the ritual that I would pass through on the way to womanhood. I tried to put the horror of it out of my mind, and as time passed, so did my memory of the agony I had witnessed on my sister's face. Finally, I foolishly convinced myself that I wanted to become a woman, too, and join my older sisters.

A friend of my father's and his family always traveled with us. He was a grouchy old man, and anytime my younger sister or I pestered him, he would wave us away as if shooing flies, and tease us by saying, "Get away from me, you two unsanitary little girls—you dirty little girls. You haven't even been circumcised yet!" He always spat the words out as if the fact we weren't circumcised made us so disgusting that he could barely stand to look at us. These insults agitated me until I vowed to find a way to make him shut his stupid mouth.

This man had a teenage son named Jamah, and I developed a crush on this boy, even though he always ignored me. Instead of me, Jamah was interested in Aman. Through time I got the idea that his preference for my older sister revolved around the fact she was superior to me since she'd been circumcised. Like his father, Jamah probably didn't want to associate with dirty, uncircumcised little girls. When I was about five years old, I went to my mother and nagged, "Mama, just find me this woman. Come on, when are you going to do it?" I thought, *I have to get it over with—get this mysterious thing done*. As my luck would have it, only a few days passed until the gypsy woman showed up again.

One evening my mother said to me, "By the way, your father ran into the gypsy woman. We're waiting for her; she should be here any day now."

The night before my circumcision, Mama told me not to drink too much water or milk, so I wouldn't have to pee-pee much. I didn't know what that meant, but didn't question her,

43

only nodded my head. I was nervous but resolved to get it over with. That evening the family made a special fuss over me and I got extra food at dinner. This was the tradition I'd witnessed through the years that made me envious of my older sisters. Just before I went to sleep, my mother said, "I'll wake you up in the morning when the time comes." How she knew when the woman was coming I have no idea, but Mama always knew these things. She simply sensed intuitively when someone was coming, or the time was right for something to happen.

I lay awake with excitement that night until suddenly Mama was standing over me. The sky was still dark, that time before dawn when the black has lightened imperceptibly to gray. She motioned for me to be silent and took my hand. I grabbed my little blanket, and still half asleep stumbled along after her. Now I know the reason they take the girls so early in the morning. They want to cut them before anybody wakes up, so nobody else will hear them scream. But at the time, even though I was confused, I simply did as I was told. We walked away from our hut, out into the brush. "We'll wait here," Mama said, and we sat down on the cold ground. The day was growing faintly lighter; I could barely distinguish shapes, and soon I heard the click-click of the gypsy woman's sandals. My mother called out the woman's name, then added, "Is that you?"

"Yes, over here," came a voice, although I still could see no one. Then, without my seeing her approach, she was right beside me. "Sit over there." She motioned toward a flat rock. There was no conversation, no hello. No "How are you?" No "What's going to happen today is going to be very painful, so you must be a brave girl." No. The Killer Woman was strictly business.

Mama grabbed a piece of root from an old tree, then positioned me on the rock. She sat behind me, and pulled my head back against her chest, her legs straddling my body. I circled my arms around her thighs. My mother placed the root between my teeth. "Bite on this."

I was frozen with fear as the memory of Aman's tortured face suddenly flooded back before me. "This is going to hurt!" I mumbled over the root.

Mama leaned over and whispered to me, "You know I can't hold you. I'm on my own here. So try to be a good girl, baby. Be brave for Mama, and it'll go fast." I peered between my legs and saw the gypsy woman getting ready. She looked like any other old Somali woman—with a colorful scarf wrapped around her head and a bright cotton dress—except there was no smile on her face. She looked at me sternly, a dead look in her eyes, then foraged through an old carpet bag. My eyes were fixed on her, because I wanted to know what she was going to cut me with. I expected a big knife, but instead, out of the bag she pulled a tiny cotton sack. She reached inside with her long fingers, and fished out a broken razor blade. Turning it from side to side, she examined it. The sun was barely up now; it was light enough to see colors but no details. However, I saw dried blood on the jagged edge of the blade. She spat on it and wiped it against her dress. While she was scrubbing, my world went dark as my mother tied a scarf around my eyes as a blindfold.

The next thing I felt was my flesh, my genitals, being cut away. I heard the sound of the dull blade sawing back and forth through my skin. When I think back, I honestly can't believe that this happened to me. I feel as if I were talking about somebody else. There's no way in the world I can explain what it feels like. It's like somebody is slicing through the meat of your thigh, or cutting off your arm, except this is the most sensitive part of your body. However, I didn't move an inch, because I remembered Aman and knew there was no escape. And I wanted Mama to be proud of me. I just sat there as if I were made of stone, telling myself the more I moved around, the longer the torture would take. Unfortunately, my legs began to quiver of their own accord, and shake uncontrollably, and I prayed, Please, God, let it be over quickly. Soon it was, because I passed out.

When I woke up, I thought we were finished, but now the worst of it had just begun. My blindfold was off and I saw the Killer Woman had piled next to her a stack of thorns from an acacia tree. She used these to puncture holes in my skin, then poked a strong white thread through the holes to sew me up. My legs were completely numb, but the pain between them was so intense that I wished I would die. I felt myself floating up, away from the ground, leaving my pain behind, and I hovered some feet above the scene looking down, watching this woman sew my body back together while my poor mother held me in her arms. At this moment I felt complete peace; I was no longer worried or afraid.

My memory ends at that instant, until I opened my eyes and the woman was gone. They had moved me, and I was lying on the ground close to the rock. My legs had been tied together with strips of cloth binding me from my ankles to my hips so I couldn't move. I looked around for my mother, but she was gone, too, so I lay there alone, wondering what would happen next. I turned my head toward the rock; it was drenched with blood as if an animal had been slaughtered there. Pieces of my meat, my sex, lay on top, drying undisturbed in the sun.

I lay there, watching the sun climb directly overhead. There was no shade around me and the waves of heat beat down on my face, until my mother and sister returned. They dragged me into the shade of a bush while they finished preparing my tree. This was the tradition; a special little hut was prepared under a tree, where I would rest and recuperate alone for the next few weeks until I was well. When Mama and Aman had finished working, they carried me inside.

I thought the agony was over until I had to pee, then I understood my mother's advice not to drink too much milk or water. After hours of waiting, I was dying to go, but with my legs tied together I couldn't move. Mama had warned me not to walk, so that I wouldn't rip myself open, because if the wound is ripped open, then the sewing has to be done again. Believe me, that was the last thing I wanted.

"I have to pee-pee," I called to my sister. The look on her face told me this was not good news. She came and rolled me over on my side and scooped out a little hole in the sand.

"Go ahead."

The first drop came out and stung as if my skin were being eaten by acid. After the gypsy sewed me up, the only opening left for urine and menstrual blood was a minuscule hole the diameter of a matchstick. This brilliant strategy ensured that I could never have sex until I was married, and my husband would be guaranteed he was getting a virgin. As the urine collected in my bloody wound and slowly trickled down my legs onto the sand—one drop at a time—I began to sob. Even when the Killer Woman was cutting me to pieces I had never cried, but now it burned so badly I couldn't take any more.

In the evening, as it grew dark, my mother and Aman returned home to the family and I stayed in the hut by myself. But this time, I wasn't scared of the dark, or the lions or the snakes, even though I was lying there helpless, unable to run. Since the moment when I floated out of my body and watched that old woman sewing my sex together, nothing could frighten me. I simply lay on the hard ground like a log, oblivious to fear, numb with pain, unconcerned whether I would live or die. I couldn't care less that everyone else was at home laughing by the fire while I lay alone in the dark.

As the days dragged on and I lay in my hut, my genitals became infected and I ran a high fever. I faded in and out of consciousness. Dreading the pain of urination, I had held back the urge to pee until my mother said, "Baby, if you don't pee, then you're going to die," so I tried to force myself. If I had to go, and no one was around, then I scooted over an inch or so, rolled myself onto my side and prepared myself for the searing pain I knew was coming. But my wound became so infected for a time that I was unable to urinate at all. Mama brought me food and water for the next two weeks; other than that I lay there alone with my legs still tied together. And waited for the wound to heal. Feverish, bored, and listless, I could do nothing but wonder: Why? What was it all for? At that age I didn't understand anything about sex. All I knew was that I had been butchered with my mother's permission, and I couldn't understand why.

Finally, Mama came for me and I shuffled home, my legs still bound together. The first night back at my family's hut, my father asked, "How does it feel?" I assume he was referring to my new state of womanhood, but all I could think about was the pain between my legs. Since I was all of five years old, I simply smiled and didn't say anything. What did I know about being a woman? Although I didn't realize it at the time, I knew a lot about being an African woman: I knew how to live quietly with suffering in the passive, helpless manner of a child.

For over a month my legs were tied together so my wound would heal. My mother constantly admonished me not to run or jump, so I shuffled along gingerly. Considering I had always been energetic and active, running like a cheetah, climbing trees, jumping over rocks, this was another kind of agony for a young girl—sitting around while all my siblings were playing. But I was so terrified of having to go through the whole process again that I barely moved an inch. Each week Mama checked me to see if I was healing properly. When the ties that bound me were removed from my legs, I was able to look at myself for the first time. I discovered a patch of skin completely smooth except for a scar down the middle like a zipper. And that zipper was definitely closed. My genitals were sealed up like a brick wall that no man would be able to penetrate until my wedding night, when my husband would either cut me open with a knife or force his way in.

As soon as I could walk again, I had a mission. I'd been thinking about it every day as I lay there, for all those weeks, ever since the day that old woman butchered me. My mission was to go back to the rock where I'd been sacrificed and search to see if my genitals were still lying there. But they were gone—no doubt eaten by a vulture or hyena, scavengers who are part of the life cycle of Africa. Their role is to clear away carrion, the morbid evidence of our harsh desert existence.

Even though I suffered as a result of my circumcision, I was lucky. Things could have been much worse, as they frequently were for other girls. As we traveled throughout Somalia, we met families and I played with their daughters. When we visited them again, the girls were missing. No one spoke the truth about their absence, or even spoke of them at all. They had died as a result of their mutilation—from bleeding to death, shock, infection, or tetanus. Considering the conditions in which the procedure is performed, that isn't surprising. What's surprising is that any of us survived.

I barely remember my sister Halemo. I was around three, and I remember her being there, then she wasn't there anymore, but I didn't understand what had happened to her. Later I learned that when her "special time" came, and the old gypsy woman circumcised her, she bled to death.

When I was around ten, I heard the story of my younger cousin's experience. At the age of six she was circumcised, and afterward one of her brothers came to stay with our family and told us what had happened. A woman came and cut his sister, then she was placed in her hut to recuperate. But her "thingy," as he called it, began to swell, and the stench coming from her hut was unbearable. At the time he told this story, I didn't believe him. Why should she smell bad, as this had never happened to me or Aman? Now I realize he was telling the truth: as a result of the filthy conditions the practice is performed in, hacking girls up in the bush, her wound became infected. The awful smell is a symptom of gangrene. One morning, their mother came in to check on her daughter who, as usual, had spent the night alone in her hut. She found the little girl lying dead, her body cold and blue. But before the scavengers could clear away the morbid evidence, her family buried her.

5.

THE MARRIAGE CONTRACT

One morning I woke to the sound of people talking. I stood up from my mat and saw no one, so I decided to investigate. Through the early stillness I tracked the voices, jogging about half a mile to where my mother and father were waving good-bye to a group of people walking away. "Who is that, Mama?" I asked, pointing at the back of a slight woman with a scarf wrapped around her head.

"Oh, that's your friend, Shukrin."

"Is her family moving from here?"

"No, she's getting married," came my mother's reply.

Stunned, I stared at the figures disappearing. I was around thirteen, and Shukrin was only slightly older than me, about fourteen, and I couldn't believe she was getting married. "To whom?" No one answered me, as such a question was considered none of my business. "To whom?" I repeated my question, which was again met by silence. "Will she be leaving here—with the man she marries?" This was common practice and my greatest fear was that I would never see my friend again.

My father said gruffly, "Don't worry about it. You're next." My parents turned and walked back to our hut, while I stood there grappling with the news. Shukrin was getting married! Married! It was a term I'd heard over and over, but until that morning I'd never really questioned what it meant.

As a girl in Somalia, I never thought about marriage or sex. In my family—in our whole culture—nobody ever talked about any of that. It never, ever, came to mind. My only thoughts on boys were competing with them to see who could be best at caring for the animals, racing with them, and beating them up. The only thing anyone ever said on the topic of sex was "Be sure you don't mess with anybody. You're supposed to be a virgin when you marry." Girls know they will marry as a virgin, and will marry only one man, and that's it. That's your life.

My father used to say to my sisters and me, "You girls are my queens," because he was considered very lucky to have some of the best-looking daughters around. "You are my queens, and no man will mess with you. If he tries, just let me know. I'm here to protect you—I'll die for you."

More than one opportunity came for him to guard his "queens." My oldest sister, Aman, was out one day taking care of her animals, when a man approached her. This guy kept pestering her, and she kept repeating, "Leave me alone. I'm not interested in you." Finally, when his charm didn't work, he grabbed Aman and tried to force himself on her. This was a big mistake, because she was an amazon, well over six feet tall, and strong as any man. She beat him up, then came home and told my father the story. My father went looking for this poor fool, then *Papa* beat him up. No man would mess with his daughters.

One night I awoke when another sister, Fauziya, let out a piercing scream. As usual we were sleeping outside under the stars, but she was separated from the rest of us, and lay off to one side. I sat up and dimly saw the shape of a man running away from our camp. Fauziya continued to scream as my father jumped up and chased the intruder. We went to her and she reached down to touch her legs, which were covered with white, sticky semen. The man escaped from my father, but in the morning, we saw the prints of the pervert's sandals next to where my sister had slept. Papa had an idea who the culprit was, but couldn't be sure.

Sometime later, during an intense dry spell, my father had traveled to a local well to gather water. As he stood in the damp earth at the bottom, a man approached. This man grew restless waiting his turn for the water and yelled out to Papa, "Hey, come on! I got to get some water, too!" In Somalia, wells are open areas where someone has dug down deep enough to reach groundwater, sometimes one hundred feet deep. As water becomes scarcer, everyone becomes very competitive, trying to get enough water for the livestock. My father replied that the gentleman should come ahead and get what he needed.

"Yeah, I will." This man wasted no time and climbed down into the hole. He went about his business, filling his bags with water, and as he walked about, my father noticed the prints of his sandals in the mud.

"It was you, wasn't it?!" Papa said, grabbing the man by the shoulders and shaking him. "You sick bastard, you're the one who was messing with my girl!" My father hit him, beating him like the cur that he was. But the cur took out a knife, a big African killer knife, carved with an ornate pattern like a ceremonial dagger. He stabbed my father four or five times in the ribs, before Papa managed to wrestle the weapon away from him and stab the man with his own knife. Now they were both seriously wounded. My father barely managed to climb out of the well, and make it back to our hut; he returned home bloody and weak. After a long illness, Papa recovered, but I realized later he had told the truth: he'd been prepared to die for my sister's honor.

———

My father always joked with us girls, "You are my queens, my treasures, and I keep you under lock and key. And I've got the key!"

I would say, "But Papa, where's the key?"

He would laugh like a madman and say, "I threw it away!"

"Well, how are we going to come out?" I would cry, and we'd all laugh.

"You're not, my darling. Not till I say you're ready."

These jokes were handed down from my oldest sister, Aman, all the way to the youngest baby girl. But they were not really jokes. Without my father's permission, there would be no access to his daughters. But more was at stake here than Papa protecting us from unwanted advances. Virgins are a hot commodity in the African marriage market, one of the largest unspoken reasons for the practice of female circumcision. My father could expect a high price for beautiful virgin daughters but had little hope of unloading one who had been soiled by having sex with another man. When I was a girl, however, none of these facts concerned me, because I was a child and never thought about the subjects of sex or marriage.

That is, until I learned of my friend Shukrin's wedding. A few days later, my father came home one evening and I heard him call out, "Hey, where's Waris?"

"Over here, Papa," I yelled.

"Come here," he called in a soft voice. Normally he was very stern and aggressive, so I knew something was up. I assumed he wanted me to do him a favor, do something with the animals tomorrow, look for water, hunt for food, or some similar chore. So I stayed where I was, staring at my father cautiously, trying to imagine what he had planned for me. "Come, come, come, come," he said impatiently.

I walked a couple of steps toward him, eyeing him suspiciously, but didn't say anything. Papa grabbed me and sat me down on his knee. "You know," he began, "you been really good." Now I *knew* something serious was up. "You been really good, more like a boy, more like a son to me." I knew this was his highest praise.

"Hmmm," I responded, wondering why I was receiving such accolades.

"You've been just like a son to me, working hard as any man, taking good care of the animals. And I just want to let you know that I'm going to miss you very much." When he said this, I thought my father was afraid that I was going to run away like my sister Aman had. When Papa had tried to arrange her marriage, she ran away. He was afraid I was going to run away, too, and leave him and Mama with all the hard work.

A flood of tenderness came over me, and I hugged him, feeling guilty for being so suspicious. "Oh, Papa, I'm not going anywhere!"

He pulled back from me, and stared at my face. In a soft voice he said, "Yes, you are, my darling."

"Where am I going? I'm not going anywhere—I'm not leaving you and Mommy."

"Yes, you are, Waris. I found you a husband."

"No, Papa, no!" I jumped up and he tried to grab me back, tried to grab my arms and hold on to me. "I don't want to leave, I don't want to leave home, I want to stay with you and Mama!"

"Sh, sh, sh, it's going to be fine. I found you a good husband."

"Who?" I said, curious now.

"You will meet him."

My eyes filled with tears, even though I tried hard to be tough. I started swinging at him, and screaming, "I don't want to get married!"

"Okay, Waris, look . . ." Papa reached down and grabbed a rock, pulled his hands behind his back, and swapped the rock back and forth. Then he held his hands out in front of him, with both fists clenched, so I couldn't see which one held the prize. "Choose the right hand or the left hand. Choose the one that holds the rock. If you guess right, you're going to do what I say and have good luck for the rest of your life. If you choose wrong, your days will be full of sorrow, because you'll be banned from the family."

I stared at him, wondering what was going to happen if I chose the wrong hand. Was I going to die? I touched his left hand. He turned up an empty palm toward the sky. "I guess I'm not going to do what you tell me," I murmured sadly.

"We can do it again."

"No." I shook my head slowly. "No, Papa. I'm not going to marry."

"He's a good man!" my father cried. "You've got to trust me—I know a good man when I see one. And you're going to do what I say!"

I stood there with my shoulders slumped, feeling sick and scared, and shook my head.

He tossed the rock hiding in his right hand into the darkness and shouted, "Then you'll have bad luck all your life!"

"Well, I guess I'm the one who'll have to live with it, won't I?" He slapped me hard across the face, because no one talked back to my father. I realize now that he had to marry me off quickly, as much for this type of behavior as for any traditional reasons. I had grown into a rebel, a tomboy, sassy and fearless, and was getting a reputation as such. Papa had to find me a husband while I was still a valuable commodity, because no African man wanted to be challenged by his wife.

The next morning I got up and took my animals out to graze as usual. While I watched them I thought about this new notion of marriage. I tried to think of a plan to persuade my father to let me remain at home, but knew in my heart this would never happen. I wondered who my new husband would be. To date, my only childish romantic inkling had been an interest in Jamah the son of my father's friend. I had seen him many times, because our families often traveled together. Jamah was considerably older than me, and I thought him very good-looking, but he wasn't married yet. My father loved him like a son, and thought Jamah was a good son to his own father. But probably my biggest attraction to Jamah was that he'd once had a serious crush on my sister Aman and didn't know I was alive. I was just a little girl to him, where Aman had been a desirable woman. When I whispered that Jamah liked her, Aman waved her hand and said, "Pshhh." She never gave him a second look, because she'd seen enough of the nomadic life and had no desire to marry a man like our father. She always talked about going to the city and marrying a man with lots of money. And when Papa tried to marry her off to one of his fellow nomads, she ran away in search of her big city dreams. We never heard from her again.

All that day, as I sat watching my animals, I tried to convince myself that marriage might not be so bad, and envisioned myself living with Jamah, the way my mother and father lived together. As the sun was going down, I walked back to our camp with my herd. My little sister ran to meet me and announced, "Papa has somebody with him and I think they're waiting for you." My sister was suspicious of this sudden interest in Waris, thinking perhaps she was being left out of some worthwhile treat. But I shuddered, knowing my father was continuing with his plan—just as if I'd never objected.

"Where are they?" My sister pointed in one direction, and I turned and headed in the other.

"Waris, they're waiting for you!" she cried.

"Oh, shut up! Get away from me!" I put my goats in their pen and began to milk them. When I was about halfway through the job, I heard my father calling my name. "Yes, Papa. I'm coming." I stood up with dread but knew there was no point in putting off the inevitable. A small hope flickered that maybe my father would be waiting with Jamah, and I envisioned his smooth handsome face. I walked toward them with my eyes closed. "Please let it be Jamah . . ." I muttered as I stumbled along. Jamah had become my salvation from this unsavory notion of leaving home to live with a strange man.

Finally, I opened my eyes and stared into the blood-red sky; the sun melted into the horizon, and I saw two men in front of me in silhouette. My father said, "Oh, there you are. Come here, my darling. This is Mr.—"; I didn't hear another word he said. My eyes fastened onto a man sitting down, holding on to a cane. He was at least sixty years old, with a long white beard.

"Waris!" I finally realized my father was talking to me. "Say hello to Mr. Galool."

"Hello," I said, in the iciest voice I could muster. I had to be respectful, but I did not have to be enthusiastic. The old fool just sat there grinning at me, leaning on his stick with all his might, but did not reply. He probably didn't know what to say, looking at this girl he was about to marry, who only stared at him in horror. To hide the look in my eyes, I hung my head down and stared at the ground.

"Now, Waris, dear, don't be shy," Papa said. I looked at my father, and when he saw my face, he realized that his best tactic was to shoo me away, so I didn't scare off my prospective husband. "Well, okay, you go ahead and finish your chores." He turned to Mr. Galool and explained, "She's just a shy, quiet young girl." I didn't linger another second but ran back to my goats.

All that evening I thought about what my life would be like married to Mr. Galool. Never having been away from my parents, I tried to imagine living not with them, but instead with a person who I didn't even know. At least it was fortunate that I didn't add to my misery by including the thought of having sex with a disgusting old man. But at the tender age of thirteen, I was naive about that part of the bargain. As a distraction to take my mind off my marriage dilemma, I beat up my little brother.

Early the next morning my father called me. "You know who that was last night?"

"I can guess."

"That's your future husband."

"But Papa, he's so old!" I still couldn't believe my father thought so little of me that he'd send me to live with an old man like that.

"That's the best kind, darling! He's too old to run around, chasing after other women, bringing home other wives. He's not going to leave you—he'll look after you. And besides"—Papa grinned proudly—"do you know how much he's paying for you?"

"How much?"

"FIVE camels! He's giving me FIVE camels." Papa patted my arm. "I'm so proud of you."

I looked away from my father, watching the golden rays of morning sun bring the desert landscape to life. Closing my eyes, I felt its warmth on my face. My thoughts returned to the previous night when I couldn't sleep. Instead, I lay there sheltered in the midst of my family, watching the stars spin overhead, and made my decision. I knew if I protested against marrying the old man, that wouldn't be the end of the situation. My father would just find another man, then another one, then another one, because he was determined to get rid of me . . . and get his camels. I nodded my head. "Well, Father, I got to take my animals out now." Papa looked at me with satisfaction, and I could read his mind: "Hey, that was much easier than I thought it would be."

As I sat watching the goats playing that day, I knew it would be the last time I looked after my father's herd. I pictured my life with the old man, the two of us in some completely isolated desert place. Me doing all the work, while he limped around with his cane. Me living alone after he had a heart attack, or better yet, me raising four or five babies alone after he died, because in Somalia, widows do not remarry. I made up my mind—this was not the life for me. That night when I came home, my mother asked me what was wrong. "Have you met that man?" I snapped.

She didn't need to ask me which man. "Yes, I saw him the other day."

In a frantic whisper, so my father couldn't hear, I said, "Mama, I don't want to marry that man!"

She shrugged. "Well, my darling, it's out of my hands. What can I do? It's your father's decision." I knew that maybe tomorrow or the next day, my new husband would come for me, bringing his five camels in exchange. I formed my plan to run away before it was too late.

That evening after everyone went to sleep, I listened for Papa's familiar snoring. Then I got up and went to my mother, who still sat next to the fire. "Mama," I whispered, "I can't marry that man—I'm going to run away."

"Shhh, quiet! Where, child? Where are you going to go?"

"I'll find Auntie in Mogadishu."

"Do you know where she is? I don't!"

"Don't worry, I'll find her."

"Well, it's dark now," she rationalized, as if this could stop destiny.

"Not now, in the morning," I whispered. "Wake me up before the sun comes up." I knew I needed her help, because it wasn't as if I could just set the alarm clock. I needed to get some rest before I set off on my long journey, but I also needed to get a head start before my father woke up.

"No." She shook her head. "It's too dangerous."

"Oh, please! Mama, I cannot marry this man—go and be his wife! Please, please. I'll come back for you. You know I will."

"Go to bed." She had that stern look, her look that told me the subject was closed. I left my tired mother looking into the fire and I pushed into the tangle of arms and legs, between my brothers and sisters, to get warm.

While I was sleeping, I felt my mother lightly tap my arm. She knelt on the ground beside me. "Go now." Immediately I was jolted awake, then flooded with the sick sensation of what I had to do. I wriggled carefully from the warm bodies and checked to make sure my father was in his usual position guarding the family. He still lay snoring.

I shivered and walked away from our hut with my mother. "Mama, thank you for waking me." In the gloomy light I struggled to see her face, trying to memorize its features, because I wouldn't see that face again for a long time. I had planned to be strong, but instead choked on my tears and hugged her hard.

"Go—go before he wakes up," she said softly into my ear. I felt her arms tighten around me. "You're going to be all right—don't you worry about that. You just be very careful. Careful!" She turned me loose. "And Waris . . . please, one thing. Don't forget me."

"I won't, Mama . . ." I spun away from her and ran into the darkness.

6.

ON THE ROAD

We'd driven only a few kilometers when the elegantly dressed man pulled his Mercedes over. "I'm afraid this is as far as I'm going. I'll let you out here so you can get another ride."

"Oh . . ." This was disappointing news indeed, since after running away from my father, walking across the desert, starving for days, being stalked by a lion, whipped by a herdsman, and attacked by a truck driver, this gentleman in the Mercedes had been the best thing that had happened to me since I left home.

"Good luck on your journey," he called from the open window and, waving, displayed his white teeth again. I stood in the sun on the side of the dusty road and waved back without much enthusiasm. I watched his car speed away into the shimmering waves of heat and started walking again, wondering if I'd ever make it to Mogadishu.

That day I got a few more rides, but they were for short distances; in between I kept walking. As the sun was going down, another big truck pulled over to the side of the road.

Frozen with fear, I stared at the red brake lights, remembering my last experience with a trucker. While I stood there thinking, the driver turned around inside the cab to look at me. If I didn't act soon, I knew he'd pull away without me, so I hurried up to the cab. The truck was a huge semi; when the driver opened the door from inside, I struggled to climb in. "Where are you headed?" he said. "I'm only going as far as Galcaio."

When the driver said "Galcaio," a great idea flashed into my mind. I hadn't realized I was close to the city, but my rich uncle lived in Galcaio. Instead of wandering all over Somalia looking for Mogadishu, I could stay with Uncle Ahmed. In my mind we still had some unfinished business anyway, because I'd never received my shoes in exchange for taking care of his animals. I imagined eating a big meal at his fine home that night and sleeping there instead of under a tree. "Yeah, that's where I'm going." I smiled, liking the idea. "I'm headed to Galcaio, too." In the back, the truck was loaded with food: heaps of yellow corn, sacks of rice and sugar. Looking at them reminded me of how hungry I was.

The truck driver was about forty, and a big flirt. He kept trying to strike up a conversation; I wanted to be friendly, but I was disgustingly scared. The last thing I wanted was for him to think I was interested in messing around with him. Looking out the window, I tried to imagine the best way to find my uncle's house, since I had no idea where he lived. But then one of the driver's comments caught my attention: "You're running away, aren't you?"

"Why do you say that?" I said in surprise.

"I can just tell—I know you are. I'm turning you in."

"What—NO! Please, please . . . I'm going. I've got to go. I just want you to take me . . . take me to Galcaio. I've got to go visit my uncle there. He's expecting me." The look on his face told me he didn't believe me, but all the same he kept driving. My mind raced ahead—where should I tell the driver to let me out? After this story, that my uncle was expecting me, I couldn't admit I didn't know where to go. As we entered the city I looked around at the streets crowded with buildings, cars, and people; this was much bigger than the village I'd encountered earlier, and for the first time I realized what I was up against trying to find Uncle.

From high up in the cab of the semi, I nervously looked down on the confusion of Galcaio. To my eyes, the city was mass chaos, and I was torn between not wanting to get out of the truck, and feeling I'd better get out damn quick before this guy decided to turn me in as a runaway. When he pulled up next to an outdoor market, and I saw the stalls full of food, I decided to go. "Hey, um, friend, I'll get out here. My uncle lives down there," I said, pointing toward a side street and jumping out the door before he could stop me. "Thanks for the lift," I called as I slammed the door.

I walked through the market in astonishment. Never, ever in my life had I seen so much food. I remember thinking how beautiful it was! Piles of potatoes, mountains of corn, racks of dried pasta. And my God, all the colors! Bins piled high with bright yellow bananas, green and golden melons, and thousands and thousands of red tomatoes. I had never seen these foods before, and I stood in front of a display of tomatoes. This moment was the beginning of my love of luscious, ripe tomatoes, and to this day I've never gotten enough of them. I stared at the food, and all the people walking through the market stared at me. The woman who owned the stand headed toward me, frowning. She was a complete mama. (In Africa, "mama" is a term of respect for women. It means you're mature, you've come of age, and in order to deserve this title you must actually be a mother.) All her colors and scarves were flashing. "What do you want?" this mama demanded.

"Please, can I have some of this?" I said, pointing to the tomatoes.

"Do you have money?"

"No, but I'm so hungry—"

"Get out of here—GO!" she cried, shooing me away from her stall with one hand.

I went to another vendor and started in again. This woman said, "I don't need any beggars hanging around in front of my place. I'm trying to run a business here. Go on, go away."

I told her my story, that I needed to find Uncle Ahmed, and asked if she knew where he lived. I assumed since my uncle was a wealthy businessman, the people of Galcaio would know him. "Look, shut up. You can't come here from out in the bush and start shouting like that. Sh-h-h-h. Have some respect, girl. You have to be quiet. *Quiet*. Don't be yelling out your family names here in public." Staring at her, I thought, *Oh, Lord, what is this woman talking about, and how am I ever going to communicate with these people?*

Off to one side of us, a man leaned against a wall. He called out, "Girl, come here." I went to him excitedly and tried to explain my predicament. The man was about thirty, a very ordinary-looking African man—nothing special—but he had a friendly face. He said patiently, "Just hush. I can help you, but you've got to be careful. You can't go around yelling out the name of your tribe like that. Now what tribe are you?" I told him all I knew about my family and Uncle Ahmed. "Okay, I think I know where he lives. Let's go and I'll help you find him."

"Oh, please—please. Can you take me there?"

"Yeah, come on. Don't worry, we'll find your man." We walked away from the busy market area, heading down one of the shady side streets. The man paused in front of a house. "Are you hungry?" This, of course, was pitifully obvious to anyone with eyes.

"Yes."

"Well, this is my house. Why don't you come in and I'll give you something to eat, then we can find your uncle?" I gratefully accepted his offer.

When we went inside, I was struck by a very peculiar smell, some strange odor that I'd never smelled before. He sat me down and brought me food. As soon as I'd taken the last bite, he said, "Why don't you come lie down with me and have a nap?"

"A nap?"

"Yeah, take a rest."

"No, please, I just want to find my uncle."

"I know, I know. But first let's have a nap. It's siesta time. Then don't worry, we'll go find him."

"No, please. You go ahead—I'll wait for you here. I don't mind." Even though it was siesta time, I had no intention of lying down with this strange man. I knew at this point that something was very, very wrong. But ignorant little girl, I didn't know what to do about it.

"Look, little girl," he said in an angry tone, "if you want me to take you to find your uncle, you better lie down and have a nap." I knew I needed this man's help to find Uncle Ahmed. And as he grew increasingly belligerent and insistent, I became frightened, so I finally did the worst possible thing I could have done. I gave in to his suggestion. Of course, the minute we lay on his bed, a nap was the last thing on his mind. In two seconds this fucking ass was trying to get on top of me. When I struggled and turned away from him, he slapped the back of my head. Don't say a word, I thought; but seizing my opportunity, I leaped from his arms and tore out of the room. As I ran, I heard him calling from his bed, "Hey, little girl, come back here . . ." Then I heard a low laugh.

I bounded onto the dark street crying hysterically and fled back to the market seeking the safety of other people. An old mama came to me, a woman about sixty years old. "Child, what's the matter?" She took my arm firmly and made me sit down. "Come, come. Talk to me—tell me what's wrong." I couldn't bring myself to admit what had just happened. I was too embarrassed and ashamed to ever tell anyone. I felt like such a fool, such a stupid little fool because I had let the whole episode happen by going into his house. Between sobs I explained to her that I was looking for my uncle, and I couldn't find him.

"Who is your uncle? What's his name?"

"Ahmed Dirie."

The old mama lifted her bony finger and pointed toward a bright blue house diagonally across the corner. "It's right there," she said. "You see that? That's your house." It was right there. All along, it was right there, across the street from where I had stood begging that bastard to help me find my uncle. Later I realized that when I was telling him my story, he knew exactly who I was, and exactly who my uncle was. The old woman asked me if I wanted her to take me there. I looked at her hard, because now I didn't trust anyone. But in her face I could see that she was a real mother.

"Yes, please," I answered faintly.

We walked across the corner and I knocked on the door of the blue house. My aunt opened the door and stared at me in shock. "What are you doing here?" The old woman turned and walked away.

"Auntie, I'm here!" I replied stupidly.

"What in Allah's name are you doing here? You ran away, didn't you!?"

"Well . . ."

"I'm taking you back," she said firmly.

Uncle Ahmed, my father's brother, was amazed to see me as well, but particularly amazed that I was able to find his house. My explanation skipped the details of clobbering a truck driver with a boulder and nearly being raped by his neighbor. However, even though he was impressed with my ability to make my way across the desert and track him down, he had no intention of letting me stay. Uncle worried about who was going to look after his animals—a task that had been my job for years, and for all my trouble he'd bought me a pair of flip-flops. All my father's older children were gone from home now. I was the oldest one left—the tough one—who was more dependable than the younger children. "No, you have to go back home. Who's going to help your mother and father with all the work? What are you going to do if you come here? Sit on your ass?" Unfortunately, I didn't have good answers for any of these questions. I knew there was no point telling him I ran away because Papa was making me marry a white-bearded old man. Uncle would look at me like I was crazy and say, "So? So? Waris, you have to get married. Your father needs the camels . . ." There was no point trying to explain that I was different from my family; I loved my parents, but what they wanted for me wasn't enough. I knew there had to be more to life, although I wasn't sure what. After a few days I learned Uncle had sent a messenger to look for my father, and Papa was on his way.

I knew Uncle Ahmed's two sons well because they used to come and stay with my family during holidays when they weren't in school. They helped us care for their animals, and taught us some Somali words. At the time, this was the tradition: the kids who went to school in town came out into the desert over break to teach the nomadic children. While I was staying with them in Galcaio, my cousins mentioned they knew where my oldest sister, Aman, was: when she ran away from home, she went to Mogadishu and got married. I was overjoyed at this news, because when she left I never heard from her again; she might as well have been dead. I realized talking to them that my parents had known where Aman was, but she'd been banned from the family, so they never spoke of her.

When I found out my father was coming to take me home, we hatched a plan. The boys gave me directions on how to find my sister once I arrived in the capital. And one morning they led me to the road out of town, then gave me what little money they had. "There you go, Waris," they said, pointing. "That's the way to Mogadishu."

"Promise me you won't tell anyone where I've gone. Remember—when my father gets here, you don't know what happened to me. The last time you saw me was this morning at the house, okay?" They nodded and waved good-bye as I started walking.

The journey to Mogadishu was excruciatingly slow. It took days, but at least now that I had a little money, I was able to buy something to eat along the way. My rides were sporadic and I walked many miles in between. Frustrated with my slow progress, I finally paid for a ride aboard an African bush taxi, a big truck with about forty people aboard. These trucks are common in Africa. After dumping their load of grain or sugarcane, they'll take passengers back in the empty trailer. Around the bed of the truck is a wooden frame like a fence; sitting or standing beside it, the people on board look like children in a gigantic playpen. The bush taxi is also crowded with babies, luggage, household goods, furniture, live goats, and crates of chickens, and the driver will pack on as many paying passengers as he can get. But after my recent experiences, I was willing to be crowded in with a large group, rather than going alone with strange men. When we got to the outskirts of Mogadishu, the truck stopped and let us off at a well where people had gathered to water their animals. I cupped some water in my hands and scooped up a drink, then splashed some on my face. I'd noticed that by this time there were many roads, since Mogadishu is the largest city in Somalia, with a population of seven hundred thousand. I approached two nomads standing with their camels and asked, "Do you know which of these roads goes to the capital?"

"Yeah, over there," the man said, pointing. I headed off in the direction he'd shown me, walking toward the interior of the city. Mogadishu is a port city on the Indian Ocean, and it was beautiful then. Walking along, I craned my neck to look at the stunning white buildings surrounded by palm trees and brightly colored flowers. Much of the architecture was built by the Italians while Somalia was an Italian colony, giving the city a Mediterranean feel. The women walking past me wore gorgeous scarves in yellow, red, and blue prints. The long scarves circled their faces, and they'd hold them under their chins as the sea breezes lifted the ends. The filmy fabric floated gracefully behind the women as they undulated down the street. I saw many Moslem women with scarves draped over their heads, the dark veils covering their faces altogether. I stared at them, wondering how they could find their way. The city sparkled in the bright sun and all the colors seemed electrified.

As I walked, I stopped people and asked directions to my sister's neighborhood. I had no street address but planned to repeat my system of finding Uncle Ahmed in Galcaio; once I got to her area, I'd go to the market and ask if anyone knew her. However, I would not be so gullible this time about letting strange men "help me."

When I arrived in the neighborhood, I quickly found a market and strolled through examining the food, deciding what I would buy with the last of my precious Somali shillings. Finally, I bought some milk at a stall run by two women; I chose them because their milk was the best price. But when I took the first sip of it, I knew something was fishy—it didn't taste right. "What's wrong with this milk?" I asked.

"Nothing! Nothing is wrong with our milk!"

"Ah, come on. One thing I know about is *milk*. It doesn't taste right. Did you put water in it or something?" Finally they admitted they mixed the milk with water so they could sell it cheaper. Their customers didn't mind. Our conversation continued and I told them I'd come to the capital to find my sister, asking if they knew Aman.

"Yeah, I thought you looked familiar!" one of the women cried. I laughed, because when we were little, I was the spitting image of my sister. They knew her because she came to that market every day. The milk lady called to her young son and told him to show me where my sister lived. "Take her to Aman's house, then come straight back here!" she commanded the boy.

We walked along the quiet streets; by now it was siesta time and people were resting from the heat of midday. The boy pointed out a tiny shack. I walked inside the house and found my sister asleep. Shaking her arm, I woke her up. "What are you doing here . . ." she said groggily, looking at me as if I were a dream. I sat down on the bed and told her my story, that I had run away just as she did many years ago. At last I had someone to talk to who I knew would understand. She would understand that at thirteen, I just couldn't bring myself to marry this stupid old man for Papa's sake.

Aman told me how she had come to Mogadishu and found her own husband. He was a good, quiet man who worked hard. She was expecting their first child, which was due in about a month. But when she stood up, she certainly didn't appear to be a woman about to give birth. At six foot two, she merely seemed tall and elegant, and in her loose African dress, she didn't even look pregnant. I remember thinking how beautiful she was, and hoped I carried my baby so well when I was expecting.

After we talked for a while, I finally worked up the courage to ask the question I'd been dying to ask: "Aman, please. I don't want to go back—can I stay here with you?"

"So you ran away and left Mama with all the work," she said sadly. But she agreed I could stay as long as I needed. Her cramped place had two rooms: a tiny one where I slept and another room she shared with her husband. We seldom saw him, however; he left in the morning and went to work, came home for lunch, took a nap, then went back to work, returning late in the evening. When he was in the house he had so little to say that I can barely remember anything about him—his name even, or what he did for a living.

Aman gave birth to a beautiful little girl and I helped take care of the baby. I also cleaned the house and carried our clothes outside and scrubbed them, hanging them on the line to dry.

I went to the market and did the shopping, learning the fine art of haggling with the vendors over prices. Mimicking the locals, I walked up to a stand and immediately demanded, "How much?" The ritual might as well have been scripted, because every day it was the same: a mama places in front of me three tomatoes, one big one and two smaller ones, and quotes me the price I'd expect to pay for three camels.

"Ah, too much," I'd respond with a bored look and a wave of my hand.

"Well, come, come, come, how much you wanna pay?"

"Two fifty."

"Oh, no, no, no! Now come *on* . . ." At this point I'd make a great show of walking away and talking to the other vendors with keen interest, always in direct view of my target. And then I'd go back and pick up where I left off, arguing until one of us got tired and gave in.

My sister constantly mentioned her concern for our mother; she worried that since I'd run away, Mama was stuck doing all the work alone. Whenever she brought up this subject, it was as if the sole blame for the situation rested on me. I shared her worry over Mama, but Aman never mentioned that *she'd* run away, also. Forgotten memories of our childhood years together came back to me now. Much had changed in the five or so years since I'd last seen her, but to Aman I was still the same goofy little sister she'd left behind; meanwhile, she would always, *always* be the oldest and the wisest. It became clear to me that even though we looked alike, our personalities were nothing alike. I grew resentful of her constant bossiness. When Papa tried to marry me off to the old man, I ran away because I thought there had to be more to life. And cooking, washing, and taking care of babies—something I'd already had plenty of with my little brothers and sisters—was not what I had in mind.

One day I left Aman's to find out what else fate had in store for me. I didn't discuss it with her; I didn't tell her I was leaving—I simply walked out one morning and never came back. It seemed like a good idea at the time, but I didn't know then that I'd never see her again.

7.

MOGADISHU

While I was living with Aman, she took me to visit some of our other relatives who were living in Mogadishu. For the first time in my life, I was able to meet some of my mother's family. She grew up in the capital with her mother, four brothers, and four sisters.

I'm grateful I got to know my grandmother while I was in Mogadishu. Today, she's around ninety years old, but when I first met her, she was in her seventies. Granny is a complete mama. Her face is light-skinned, and shows that she's a tough cookie, a woman of character and strong will. Her hands look like she's been digging in the earth so long that they've developed crocodile hide.

My grandmother grew up in one of the Arab countries, but I don't know which. She's a devout Moslem, prays five times a day facing Mecca, and always wears a dark veil over her face when she leaves the house; she's covered up from head to toe. I used to tease her: "Granny, are you okay? You sure you know where you're going? Can you see through that thing?"

"Oh, come, come, come," she'd bark. "This thing is completely see-through."

"Good—so you can breathe and everything?" I'd laugh.

Staying at my grandmother's house, I realized where Mama got her strength. My grandfather had been dead many years, and Granny lived alone, taking care of everything by herself. And when I went to visit her, she'd wear me out. As soon as we got up in the morning she was ready to go. She'd start in on me right away: "Get going. Come on, Waris. Let's go."

Granny lived in a neighborhood of Mogadishu that was a good distance from the market. Each day we'd shop for food, and I'd say, "Come on, Granny—let's take it easy and ride the bus. It's hot and the market's too far from here to walk."

"What!? *Bus!* Now, come, come, come. Let's go. Young girl like you, wanting to take the bus. What are you complaining about? You're getting lazy these days, Waris. All you children today—I don't know what's wrong with you. When I was your age, oh, I'd walk for miles and miles . . . girl, are you coming with me or not?" So off we went together, because if I dawdled, she was obviously going to go without me. On the way home, I'd come trudging along behind her, carrying the bags.

After I left Mogadishu, one of my mother's sisters died, leaving nine children. My grandmother took care of these kids, raising them just as she did her own. She's a mama and she did what had to be done.

I met another one of her sons, Mama's brother Wolde'ab. I had gone to the market one day, and when I returned, he was sitting at my grandmother's with one of my cousins on his lap. Even though I'd never seen him before, I ran to him, because suddenly here was this man who looked exactly like my mother—and I was desperate for anything that reminded me of Mama. I ran to him, and since I also look very much like my mother, it was a wonderful but strange moment, like looking in some sort of crazy, distorted mirror. He had heard that I'd run away and was staying in Mogadishu. As I came closer to him, he said, "Is this who I think it is?" That afternoon I laughed more than I had since I left home, because not only did Uncle Wolde'ab look like my mother, he had her silly sense of humor. The brother and sister must have been quite a team growing up, cracking everyone in the family up till they cried, and I wish I could have seen them together.

But it was to Aunt L'uul's home that I went the morning I ran away from my sister's. Shortly after I arrived in Mogadishu, we had gone there together for a visit. The day I left Aman's, I decided that I would go to Aunt L'uul's house and ask if I could stay with her. She was my aunt by marriage, since she was married to my mother's brother, Uncle Sayyid. However, she spent her days raising their three children alone, as he was living in Saudi Arabia. Because the economy in Somalia was so poor, Uncle worked in Saudi and sent money back home to support his family. Unfortunately, he was away the whole time I lived in Mogadishu, so I never got to meet him.

When I arrived, Aunt L'uul was surprised, but she seemed genuinely glad to see me. "Auntie, things aren't working out very well between Aman and me, and I wondered if I could stay here with you for a while."

"Well, yes, you know I'm here by myself with the children. Sayyid is gone most of the time and I could use a hand. That would be nice." Immediately I felt relieved; Aman had grudgingly let me stay with her, but I knew she didn't like the situation. Her place was too tiny, and she was still a relative newlywed. Besides, what she really wanted was for me to go back home, to ease her conscience about running away from Mama all those years ago.

Staying first at Aman's, then Auntie L'uul's, I got accustomed to life indoors. At first, the confinement of living in a house seemed strange to me—having my view of the sky blocked by a ceiling, the space I could move around in limited by walls, the brush and animal smells of the desert replaced by the sewage and carbon monoxide smells of a crowded city. Auntie's place was somewhat bigger than Aman's, but still not spacious by any means. And even though the facilities offered me new luxuries—keeping warm at night and dry when it rained—they were primitive by contemporary Western standards. My respect for water continued, as it remained a precious commodity. We purchased it from a vendor who transported his wares through the neighborhood by donkey, then we stored the water outside in a barrel. The family dipped it out sparingly for bathing, cleaning, making tea, cooking. In the small kitchen, Auntie prepared meals on a camp stove using bottled gas. In the evening, we sat around the house and talked by kerosene lamps, as there was no electricity. The toilet was typical of this part of the world: a hole in the floor where the waste fell and remained stinking in the heat. Bathing meant carrying a bucket of water in from the barrel outside, and sponging off, letting the excess run down the hole into the toilet.

Soon after I arrived at Auntie L'uul's, I realized I was getting more than I'd bargained for when I asked for a place to stay. I was also getting a full-time job as baby-sitter for her three rotten children. Well, I guess I couldn't really categorize the little baby as rotten, but its behavior distressed me all the same.

Each morning Auntie got up around nine, and right after breakfast she gleefully left the house to visit her friends. Then she spent the entire day with these women, gossiping endlessly about their friends, enemies, acquaintances, and neighbors. Eventually she meandered back home in the evening. While she was gone, the three-month-old baby cried constantly, wanting to be fed. When I held it, it started sucking me. Every day I would say, "Look, Auntie—for God's sake—you've got to do something. The baby's trying to suck me every time I pick it up, and I don't have any milk. I don't even have any breasts!"

"Well, don't worry. Just give him some milk," she said pleasantly.

Besides cleaning the house, and taking care of the baby, there was a nine-year-old and a six-year-old to look after. And these two were like wild animals. They had no idea how to behave, because obviously their mother never taught them anything. I tried to rectify this situation immediately by whipping their ass every chance I got. But after years of running around like hyenas, they were not going to become little angels over night.

As the days passed, I got more and more frustrated. I wondered how many more of these hopeless situations I was going to have to go through before something positive happened. I was always looking for a way to make things better, push myself forward, and find whatever that mysterious opportunity was that I knew was waiting for me. Every day I wondered, "When is it going to happen? Is it today? Tomorrow? Where am I going to go? What am I going to do?" Why I thought this, I've never known. I guess at that time I thought everyone had these voices inside them. But as far back as I can remember, I always knew my life was going to be different from those around me; I just had no idea how different.

My stay with Aunt L'uul reached a crisis after I'd been there about a month. Late one afternoon, as Auntie was off making her rounds of the gossip mill, the oldest child, her nine-year-old daughter, disappeared. First I went outside and called her. When she didn't reply, I started walking through the neighborhood looking for her. Finally, I found her in a tunnel with a young boy. She was a strong-minded, inquisitive child, and by the time I caught up to her, she had become very inquisitive about this little boy's anatomy. I marched into the tunnel, grabbed her arm, and jerked her to her feet; the boy took off running like a frightened animal. All the way back to the house I whipped my cousin with a switch, as I had never been so disgusted with a child in my life.

That evening when her mother came home, the daughter cried about the spanking I had given her. Aunt L'uul was furious. "Why are you spanking this child?" she demanded. "You keep your hands off my baby or I'm going to beat you up and see how you like it!" she shouted, and came toward me menacingly.

"Believe me, you don't want to know the reason I spanked her, because you don't want to know what I know! If you had seen what she did today, you would say she's no daughter of yours. This child is out of control—she's like an animal." My explanation did not make matters any better between the two of us. Suddenly after leaving me—a thirteen-year-old girl—to cope with three children under the age of ten, her daughter's welfare was of major importance to her. My aunt came at me shaking her fist, threatening to beat me for what I'd done to her little angel. But I'd had enough—not only from her, but from the whole world. "Look, you're not going to touch me!" I screamed. "If you do, you're going to wind up bald-headed." This ended any discussion of anyone beating me, but I knew at this point I had to go. But where would I run to this time?

Raising my fist to knock on Aunt Sahru's door, I thought, *Here we go again, Waris.* Sheepishly, I said hello when she answered the door. Auntie Sahru was Mama's sister. And she had five children. This fact, I felt, did not bode well for my happiness in her household, but what choice did I have? Become a pickpocket or beg for food on the street? Without going into details about my departure from Auntie L'uul's, I asked if I could stay with her family for a while.

"You have a friend here," she said to my surprise. "If you want to stay with us, you can. If you want to talk about anything, I'm here." Things were off to a better start than I'd imagined. As expected, I began helping around the house. But Auntie Sahru's oldest daughter, Fatima, was nineteen years old. The majority of the responsibility for running the house fell to her.

My poor cousin Fatima worked like a slave. She got up early each day and went to college, then came home at twelve-thirty to cook lunch, returned to school and came back again around six in the evening to make dinner. After dinner she would clean up, then study late into the night. For some reason her mother treated her differently, demanding much more from her than she did from any of the other children. But Fatima was good to me; she treated me like a friend, and at that time in my life I certainly needed one. However, the way she was treated by her mom seemed unfair to me, so I tried to help my cousin in the kitchen at night. I didn't know how to cook, but I tried to learn by watching her. The first time I ever tasted pasta was when Fatima made it, and I thought I was in heaven.

My responsibilities were largely cleaning, and to this day Auntie Sahru says I'm the best cleaner she ever had. I scrubbed and polished the house, which was hard work. But I definitely preferred cleaning to baby-sitting, especially after my adventures of the past few months.

Like Aman, Auntie Sahru continued to worry about my mother, and the fact that Mama was left without any older girls to help her with the work. My father might help with the animals, but he wouldn't lift a finger to help with the cooking, or clothing, or making baskets, or taking care of the children. This was woman's work, and Mama's problem. After all, hadn't he done his part by bringing home another wife to help? Yes, he certainly had. But I, too, had been worried about this issue since the dark morning when I last saw my mother. Whenever I thought of her, I remembered her face in the firelight the night before I left, and how tired she'd looked. While I was running across the desert looking for Mogadishu, I couldn't get these thoughts out of my mind. The journey had seemed as endless as my dilemma: Which would I chose—my desire to take care of my mother or my desire to be rid of the old man? I remember collapsing under a tree at dusk and thinking, *Who's going to look after Mama now? She's going to look after everyone else, but who's going to look after her?*

There was no point in turning back now, however; it would simply mean I had gone through all the hardships of the past few months for nothing. If I went back home, a month wouldn't pass before my father started dragging around every lame, decrepit fool in the desert who owned a camel, trying to marry me off. Then not only would I be stuck with a husband, I still wouldn't be there to take care of my mother. But one day I decided that a partial remedy for this problem was to earn some money and send it to her. Then she could buy some of the things my family needed and wouldn't have to work so hard.

I set out to find a job, and began looking all over the city. One day my aunt sent me to the market to do her shopping, and on the way home I passed a construction site. I stopped and watched the men carrying bricks, mixing pits of mortar by tossing in shovels of sand and stirring in water with a hoe. "Hey," I yelled out, "do you have any jobs?"

The guy laying bricks stopped and started laughing at me. "Who wants to know?"

"I do. I need a job."

"Nope. We don't have any work for a skinny girl like you. Somehow I don't think you're a bricklayer." He laughed again.

"Hey, you're wrong," I assured him. "I can do it—I'm very strong. Really." I pointed at the guys mixing the mortar; they stood there with their pants hanging down to their buttocks. "I can help them. I can bring all the sand, and mix as good as they can."

"Okay, okay. When can you start?"

"Tomorrow morning."

"Be here at six and we'll see what you can do." I floated back to Auntie Sahru's without touching the ground. I had a job! I would be earning money—real cash! And I would save every penny and send it to Mama. She'd be so surprised.

When I got to the house, I told Auntie my news. She couldn't believe it. "You got a job *where?*" First of all, she couldn't believe any girl would want to do this kind of work. "And exactly what are you going to do for these men?" she asked. Second, she couldn't believe the boss would hire a female, especially me, as I still looked half-starved. But when I insisted it was true, she had no choice but to believe me.

Once she believed me, she was angry that I planned to live with her, yet instead of helping out with the household chores, I'd be working for someone else. "Look," I said tiredly. "I need to send Mama money, and in order to do that, I have to get a job. Either it's this one, or a different one, but all the same, I have to do it. Okay?"

"All right."

The next morning my career as a construction worker began. And it was horrible. I struggled carrying back-breaking loads of sand all day; I didn't have any gloves, the bucket handle cut into my hands. Then, along my palms, I developed enormous blisters. By the end of the day the blisters had burst and my hands were bleeding. Everyone thought that was the end of me, but I was determined to come back the next morning.

I stuck it out for a month, before my hands were so torn up and sore that I could barely bend them. But by the time I quit, I had saved the equivalent of sixty dollars. I told my auntie proudly that I had saved some money to send home to Mama. Recently a man she knew had visited us; he was soon heading out into the desert with his family and offered to take the money to my mother. Auntie Sahru said, "Yeah, I know his people; they're all right. You can trust them to take the money." Needless to say, that was the end of my sixty dollars. After all that, I found out later that my mother never saw a penny of it.

When I retired from construction work, I started cleaning house for my aunt again. Not long after this, I was working one day as usual, when a distinguished guest arrived: the Somalian ambassador to London. The ambassador, Mohammed Chama

Farah, happened to be married to yet another aunt, my mother's sister Maruim. As I dusted my way around the next room, I overheard the ambassador talking to Auntie Sahru. He had come to Mogadishu to find a servant before he began his four-year diplomatic appointment in London. Instantly, I knew this was it. This was the opportunity I had been waiting for.

Bursting into the room, I called to Aunt Sahru, "Auntie, I need a conversation."

She looked at me in exasperation. "What is it, Waris?"

"Please—in here." When she walked through the door and out of his sight, I grabbed hold of her arm fiercely. "Please. Please tell him to take me. I can be his maid." She looked at me and I could see the hurt on her face. But I was a strong-willed kid only thinking about what I wanted, instead of what she'd done for me.

"You! You don't know nothing about nothing. What are you going to do in London?"

"I can clean! Tell him to take me to London, Auntie! I want to GO!"

"I don't think so. Now, stop bothering me and get to work." She walked back into the other room and sat beside her brother-in-law. I heard her say quietly, "Why don't you take her? You know—she really is good. She's a good cleaner."

Auntie called me into the room and I leaped through the door. I stood there with my feather duster in my hand, smacking my gum. "I'm Waris. You're married to Auntie, aren't you?"

The ambassador frowned at me. "Would you mind taking that chewing gum out of your mouth?" I spat the wad into the corner. He looked at Auntie Sahru. "This is the girl? Oh, no, no, no."

"I'm excellent. I can clean, I can cook—and I'm good with children, too!"

"Oh, I'm sure you are."

I turned to Auntie. "Tell him—"

"Waris, that's enough. Get back to work."

"Tell him I'm the best!"

"Waris! Shush!" To my uncle she said, "She's young still, but she really is a hard worker. Believe me, she'll be okay . . ."

Uncle Mohammed sat still for a moment looking at me with disgust. "Okay, listen. I'm taking you tomorrow. Okay? I'll be here in the afternoon with your passport, then we'll go to London."

8.

GOING TO LONDON

London! I didn't know anything about it, but I liked the sound of it. I didn't know where it was, but I knew it was very far away. And far away was where I wanted to be. It seemed like the answer to my prayers, and yet too good to be true. I wailed, "Auntie, am I really going?"

She wagged her finger at me sternly. "You shut up. Don't start." When she saw the look of panic on my face, she smiled. "All right. Yes, you're really going."

On fire with excitement, I ran to tell my cousin Fatima, who was just starting dinner. "I'm going to London! I'm going to London!" I shouted and began to dance in circles around the kitchen.

"What? London!" She grabbed my arm in midspin and made me explain. "You're going to be white," Fatima announced matter-of-factly.

"What did you say?"

"You're going to be white, you know . . . *white*."

I did not know. I had no idea what she was talking about,

since I had never seen a white person, and in fact didn't know such a thing existed. However, her comment didn't trouble me in the slightest. "Shut up, please," I said in my most superior fashion. "You're just jealous that I'm going to London and you're not." I resumed my dancing, swaying and clapping my hands as if I were celebrating the rain, then chanted, "I'm going to London! Ohhh-aiyeee—I'm going to London!"

"WARIS!" Aunt Sahru called in a threatening tone.

That evening Auntie outfitted me for my journey; I received my first pair of shoes—fine leather sandals. On the plane I wore a long, brightly colored dress she'd given me, covered by a loose African robe. I had no luggage, but it didn't matter because I had nothing to take, except the outfit I'd be wearing when Uncle Mohammed picked me up the next day.

As we left for the airport, I hugged and kissed Auntie Sahru, dear Fatima, and all my little cousins good-bye. Fatima had been so kind to me that I wanted to take her with me. But I knew there was only a job for one person, and since that was the case, I was glad it was me. Uncle Mohammed gave me my passport and I looked at it in wonder—my first official document—since I had never owned a birth certificate, or any paper with my name on it. Getting into the car, I felt very important and waved farewell to the family.

Before this day I had seen airplanes from the ground; occasionally I would even see them fly overhead in the desert when I was out tending my goats, so I knew such things existed. But I certainly had never seen one up close until the afternoon I left Mogadishu. Uncle Mohammed walked me through the airport, and we paused at the door leading outside to the plane. On the tarmac, I saw a gigantic British jet gleaming in the African sun. It was at this point I heard my uncle jabbering something about ". . . and your Aunt Maruim is expecting you in London; I'll join you in a few days. I've got some business to finish up here before I can leave."

My mouth gaped as I turned around to stare at him. He thrust the plane ticket into my hand. "Now, don't lose your ticket—or your passport—Waris. These are very important documents, so hang on to them."

"You're not coming with me?" It was all I could do to choke out these words.

"No," he said impatiently, "I have to stay here for a few more days." I immediately started to cry, scared of going alone, and now that leaving Somalia was imminent, I wasn't sure it was such a good idea after all. For all its problems, it was the only home I'd ever known, and what waited ahead of me was a complete mystery.

"Go on—you'll be fine. Somebody's going to meet you in London; they'll tell you what to do when you get there." I snuffled and let out a little whimper. Uncle pushed me gently toward the door. "Go on now, the plane is leaving. Just get on . . . GET ON THE PLANE, WARIS."

Stiff with dread I walked across the sizzling tarmac. I studied the ground crew scurrying around the jet, preparing for takeoff. My eyes followed men loading luggage, the crew checking the plane, then I looked up the stairs, wondering how I was supposed to get inside this thing. Deciding on the stairs, I started up. But unused to walking in shoes, I had to struggle to make it up the slick aluminum steps without tripping over my long dress. Once on board, I had no idea where to go, and must have looked like a perfect idiot. All the other passengers were already seated, and as they sat looking at me inquiringly, I could read their faces: "Who on earth is this dumb country girl who doesn't even know how to travel on an airplane?" I spun around just inside the door and sat in an empty seat.

This was the first time I ever saw a white person. A white man sitting next to me said, "This is not your seat." At least I assume that's what he said, since I spoke not one word of English. Staring at him in panic, I thought, *Oh, Lord. What is this man saying to me? And why does he look like that?* He repeated his statement, and I repeated my panic. But then, thank God, the flight attendant came and took the ticket from my hand. Obviously, this woman knew that I was completely clueless. She took my arm and led me down the aisle to my seat—which was certainly not in first class, where I'd originally deposited myself. As I passed, each face turned to stare at me. The attendant smiled and pointed to my seat. I flopped down, grateful to be out of view; with a goofy grin, I jerked my head at her by way of saying thanks.

Shortly after takeoff, the same flight attendant returned with a basket of sweets, which she held out to me with a smile. I took one hand and picked up the fold of my dress to make a pouch, as if I were gathering fruit, and with the other, grabbed a huge handful of candy. I was famished, so I planned to load up. Who knew when I'd see any more food? As my hand came back for a second swipe, the attendant tried to move the candy out of my reach. I stretched, grabbing at the basket as she moved it farther and farther away. Her face said, "Oh, my. What am I going to do with this one?"

While I unwrapped and devoured my candy, I examined the white people around me. They looked cold and sickly to me. "You need sun," I would have said to them if I had known English; I assumed this problem was a temporary condition. They couldn't always look like that, could they? These people must have turned white because they'd been out of the sun too long. Then I decided I wanted to touch one of them the first chance I got, because maybe the white would rub off. Perhaps underneath they were really black.

After about nine or ten hours on the plane, I was desperate to pee. I was absolutely bursting, but I had no idea where to go. I thought, come on, Waris, you can figure this out. So I watched closely how all the people sitting around me got up and went to this one door. This must be it, I reasoned. I got up, and went to the door just as someone else was coming out. Once inside, I closed the door, and looked around. This has to be the right place, but where's the right spot? I looked at the sink, but disregarded it. I examined the seat, sniffed, and decided this was the right spot for my business. Happily, I sat down and—phew!

I was greatly relieved until I stood up and realized that my pee-pee was just sitting there. Now what do I do? I didn't want to leave it there for the next person to come in and see it. But how do I get it out of there? I couldn't speak English—or read—so the word *Flush* printed over the button meant nothing to me. And even if I'd understood the word, I'd never seen a flush toilet in my life. Studying every lever, knob, and screw in the room, I wondered if *this one* was the right one to make my urine disappear. Time after time, I returned to the flush button, as it seemed the obvious choice. But I was afraid if I pushed it, the plane would blow up. In Mogadishu, I'd heard of such things happening. With the constant political fighting there, people talked of bombs and explosions, blowing up this and blowing up that. Maybe if I pressed this button, the whole plane would explode and we'd all die. Maybe that's what this button said; it warned: DO NOT PRESS! WILL BLOW UP PLANE. Best not to chance it over a little pee-pee, I decided. Still, I didn't want to leave the traces of my business for others to find. And I knew they'd know exactly who left it, because by now, they were all outside pounding on the door.

In a flash of inspiration I grabbed up a used paper cup and filled it from the drizzling faucet. I poured this into the toilet, reasoning if I diluted the urine enough, the next person in would think this bowl was simply full of water. Steadily I set to work, filling the cup and pouring, filling the cup and pouring. By now, people were not only pounding on the door, they were shouting, too. And I couldn't even answer them with "Just a minute . . ." So, in silence, I kept working at my plan, filling up the soggy cup from the dripping faucet, and pouring it into the toilet bowl. I stopped when the water level was right under the rim of the seat; I knew if I added another drop, it was going to pour out onto the floor. But at least the contents looked like ordinary water, so I stood up, smoothed down my dress, and opened the door. Looking down, I pushed past the throng gathered outside, grateful that at least I hadn't poo-pooed.

When we landed at Heathrow, my fear at coping with the strange country was outweighed by my relief to get off that plane. At least Auntie would be there to greet me, and I was thankful for that. As the plane descended, the sky outside the window changed from foamy white clouds to a gray blur. When the other passengers stood up, I stood up, and let myself be swept along in the tide of bodies exiting the plane, with no idea of where to go, what to do. The crowd pushed forward until we reached a set of stairs. There was only one problem: the stairs were moving. I stopped cold, watching them. The sea of people parted around me, and I watched them smoothly step on the moving stairs and rise to the top. Mimicking them, I stepped forward too, and boarded the escalator. But one of my new sandals slipped off and stayed on the floor. "My shoe! My shoe!" I cried in Somali and rushed back to retrieve it. But the mob packed on behind me wouldn't let me pass.

When we got off the escalator, I limped along with the crowd, wearing only one sandal. Next we reached customs. I looked at the white men in their very proper British uniforms—only I had no idea who these people were. A customs official spoke to me in English, and seizing my chance for assistance, I gestured back toward the escalator, shouting in Somali, "My shoe! My shoe!"

He glared at me steadily with a bored, long-suffering expression, and repeated his question. I giggled nervously, temporarily forgetting my shoe. The official pointed at my passport, and I handed it to him. After examining it closely, he stamped it and waved me through.

Outside customs, a man in a chauffeur's uniform walked up to me and asked in Somali, "Are you here to work for Mr. Farah?"

I was so relieved to find someone who could speak my language, I cried ecstatically, "Yes! Yes! That's me, I'm Waris." The driver started to lead me away, but I stopped him. "My shoe, we have to go downstairs and get my shoe."

"Your shoe?"

"Yes, yes, it's back there."

"Where is it?"

"It's at the bottom of those moving stairs." I pointed in the opposite direction. "I lost it when I got on." He looked down at my one sandaled foot and one bare foot.

Luckily, the driver also spoke English, so he got permission for us to reenter the gate and fetch my missing sandal. But when we reached the point where I'd left my shoe, there was no sign of it. I couldn't believe my bad luck. I took off my other sandal and carried it in my hand, scanning the floor as we came back upstairs. But now I had to go through customs all over again. This time the same official got to ask me the questions he'd wanted to ask the first time around, by using the chauffeur to translate.

"How long are you staying?" the customs man asked me. I shrugged. "Where are you going?"

"To live with my uncle, the ambassador," I said proudly.

"Your passport says you're eighteen; is that correct?"

"Huh? I am not eighteen!" I protested to the driver. He translated to the customs man.

"Do you have anything to declare?" This question I didn't understand.

The driver explained, "What are you bringing with you into the country?" I held up my one sandal. The customs official stared at my shoe for a minute, then shaking his head slightly, returned my passport and flagged us through.

As the driver led me out of the crowded airport, he

explained, "Look, your passport says you're eighteen, so that's what I told the man. If anyone asks you, you should say you're eighteen."

"I am NOT eighteen," I said angrily. "That's old!"

"Well, how old are you?"

"I don't know—maybe fourteen—but I'm not *that* old!"

"Look, that's what your passport says, so that's how old you are now."

"What are you talking about? I don't care what my passport says—why does it say that, when I'm telling you it's not true?"

"Because that's what Mr. Farah told them."

"Well, he's crazy! He doesn't know anything!" By the time we reached the exit we were shouting and Uncle Mohammed's chauffeur and I had developed a hearty dislike for each other.

As I walked out to the car barefoot, snow was falling on London. I put my one sandal back on and shivered, pulling my thin cotton robe around me. I had never experienced weather like this before, and had certainly never seen snow. "Oh, my God—it's so cold here!"

"Get used to it."

As the driver eased the car out of the airport and into the London morning traffic, I was overcome by such a sad, lonely feeling, in this completely foreign place, with nothing but white sickly faces around me. Allah! Heaven! Mama! Where am I? At that moment I desperately wanted my mother. Even though he had the only other black face around, Uncle Mohammed's chauffeur was no comfort to me; obviously he considered me beneath him.

While driving, he filled me in on the household I was joining: I'd be living there with my uncle and aunt, Uncle Mohammed's mother, another uncle I hadn't met—one of my mother and Aunt Maruim's brothers, and the seven children, my cousins. After he told me who lived in the house, he informed me when I would get up, when I would go to bed, what I would be doing, what I would be cooking, where I would sleep, when I would go to bed, and how I'd fall into that bed exhausted at the end of each day.

"You know, your aunt, the mistress, runs this household with an iron fist," he confided matter-of-factly. "I warn you, she gives everybody a hard time."

"Well, she may give *you* a hard time, but she's *my* aunt." After all, she's a woman and my mother's sister, I reasoned. I thought of how much I missed Mama, and how good Auntie Sahru and Fatima had been to me. Even Aman had meant well, but we just couldn't get along. The women in the family cared, and looked after each other. I leaned back against the seat, suddenly very tired after my long journey.

I squinted out the car window, trying to see where the white flakes came from. The snow was gradually turning the sidewalks white as we glided through the posh residential section of Harley Street. When we stopped in front of my uncle's home, I stared at the house in astonishment, realizing that I was going to live in this grand place. In my limited experience in Africa, I'd never seen anything like it. The ambassador's residence was a four-story mansion, and it was yellow, my favorite color. We walked to the front door, an impressive entrance with a fanlight above. Inside the door, a large gilt-framed mirror reflected a solid wall of books from the library opposite.

Auntie Maruim walked into the foyer to greet me. "Auntie!" I cried.

A woman slightly younger than my mother, wearing stylish Western clothes, stood in the hall. "Come in," she said coolly. "Close the door." I had planned to rush to her and hug her, but something about the way she stood there with her hands pressed together made me freeze in the doorway. "First I'd like to show you around and explain what your duties are."

"Oh," I said quietly, feeling the last spark of energy leave my body. "Auntie, I'm very tired. I just want to lie down. Can I please go to sleep now?"

"Well, yes. Come with me." She walked into the living room, and as we climbed the stairs, I saw the elegant furnishings: the chandelier, white sofa covered with dozens of pillows, abstract oils hanging over the mantel, the logs crackling in the fireplace. Aunt Maruim took me into her room and told me I could sleep in her bed. The four-poster was the size of my family's entire hut and was covered with a beautiful down comforter. I ran my hand across the silky fabric, enjoying its feel. "When you wake up, I'll show you the house."

"Are you going to wake me up?"

"No. You wake up when you wake up. Sleep as long as you like." I climbed under the covers and thought I had never felt anything so soft and heavenly in my life. Auntie closed the door quietly, and I fell asleep as if I were falling down a tunnel—a long black tunnel.

9.

THE MAID

When I opened my eyes, I thought I was still dreaming—and it was a beautiful dream. Waking up in the huge bed in the lovely room, at first I couldn't believe it was real. Aunt Maruim must have slept with one of the children that night, because I lay unconscious in her room until the following morning. But as soon as I got out of bed, my fantasy life crashed back to real life.

I came out of Auntie's room, and was wandering through the house when she found me. "Good. You're up. Let's go to the kitchen and I can show you what you'll be doing." In a daze, I followed her into the room she called the kitchen; however, it did not look like the kitchen in my auntie's house in Mogadishu. The room was surrounded by creamy-white cabinets, gleamed with blue ceramic tiles, and was dominated in the center by a monstrous six-burner stove. Auntie opened and slammed drawers, calling out, ". . . and here are the utensils, the cutlery, the linens . . ." I had no idea what this woman was talking about—no idea what these things were she was showing me, let alone what I was supposed to do with them. "At six-thirty each morning you'll serve your uncle's breakfast, because he goes to the embassy early. He's a diabetic, so we must watch his diet carefully. He always has the same thing: herbal tea and two poached eggs. I'd like my coffee in my room at seven; then you'll make pancakes for the children; they eat at eight sharp, because they have to be at school by nine. After breakfast—"

"Auntie, how am I supposed to know how to do all these things? Who's going to teach me? I don't know how to make— how you call it—pancakes. What's pancakes?"

Aunt Maruim had just inhaled a big breath before I interrupted her, and she'd extended her arm pointing at a door. She held the breath for a moment with her arm still outstretched, while she stared at me with sort of a panicky look on her face. Then she exhaled slowly and brought her arm down to her side, pressing her hands together the way she had when I first saw her. "I'll do these things the first time, Waris. But you must watch me closely. Watch me very closely, listen, and learn." I nodded, and she inhaled again, picking up where she'd left off.

After the first week, and a few minor disasters, I had the routine down to a science and followed it every day, 365 days a year, for the next four years. For a girl who had never been aware of time, I learned to watch the clock closely—and live by it. Up at six, Uncle's breakfast at six-thirty, Auntie's coffee at seven, children's breakfast at eight. Then I cleaned the kitchen. The chauffeur brought the car back from taking my uncle to the embassy, and took the children to school. Then I cleaned my aunt's room, then her bathroom, then worked through each room of the house, dusting, mopping, scrubbing, and polishing my way up all four floors. And believe me, if I didn't clean the house to someone's satisfaction, I heard about it. "I don't like the way you cleaned the bathroom. Make sure it's clean, next time. This white tile should be spotless—shining."

Other than the chauffeur and the chef, I was the only servant for the entire household; my aunt explained there was no need to hire more help for a small place like ours. Chef made dinner only six nights a week, and on Sunday, his day off, I cooked. In four years I never had a day off. The few times I asked, my aunt threw such a fit that I gave up trying.

I didn't eat with the family. I grabbed something when I had a chance, and kept working until I fell into bed around midnight. But I didn't feel that missing dinner with the family was any great loss, because in my opinion, the chef's cooking was garbage. He was a Somali, but from a different tribe than mine. I thought he was a pompous, wicked, lazy man, who loved to torment me. Whenever my aunt would walk into the kitchen, he would start in out of the blue: "Waris, when I came back in on Monday morning, you had left the kitchen in a disgusting mess. It took me hours to clean it." Of course this was a total lie. All he ever studied were ways to make himself look good in front of my aunt and uncle, and he knew it wasn't going to be with his food. I told my aunt I didn't want to eat her chef's cooking, and so she said, "Well, make whatever you want, then." At this point I was really glad I had watched my cousin Fatima cook back in Mogadishu. But intuitively I had a talent for cooking and began making pasta dishes and creating all sorts of things strictly out of my imagination. When the family saw what I was eating, they wanted some too. Soon they were asking me what I'd like to make, what ingredients I needed from the market, and so on. This did nothing to increase my popularity with Chef.

By the end of my first week in London, I realized that I and my aunt and uncle held two vastly different notions of the role I'd play in their lives. Throughout most of Africa it's common for more affluent family members to take in the children of their poor relations, and those children work in return for their upkeep. Sometimes the relatives educate the children and treat them like one of their own. Sometimes they don't. Obviously I was hoping my situation would fall into the former category, but soon I learned that my aunt and uncle had more important issues on their minds than cultivating this ignorant child they'd received from the desert who was supposed to perform as a maid. Uncle was so busy with his work that he paid little attention to what went on at home. But my auntie, who I had fantasized would be like a second mother to me, apparently had no such fantasies about making me a third daughter. I was simply a servant. As this fact became brutally clear, along with the drudgery of my long workdays, my joy at coming to London withered. I discovered that my aunt was obsessed with rules and regulations; everything must always be done exactly the way she said, at exactly the time she said, every day. No exceptions. Perhaps she felt she needed to be rigid in order to succeed in this foreign culture so different from our homeland. However, fortunately, I found a friend in the house in my cousin Basma.

Basma was my uncle and aunt's oldest daughter, and we were the same age. She was stunning, and all the boys were after her, but she paid no attention. She went to school, and at night the only thing she was interested in was reading. My cousin would go to her room and lie across the bed reading for hours. Frequently she would be so engrossed in a book that she would miss meals, sometimes for the whole day until someone dragged her out of her room.

Bored and lonely, I would go into Basma's room to visit, and sit down on a corner of her bed. "What are you reading?" I'd ask.

Without looking up she'd mumble, "Leave me alone. I'm reading. . . ."

"Well, can't I talk to you?"

Still staring at the book, she'd respond in a flat voice, slurring her words, as if she were talking in her sleep, "What do you want to talk about?"

"What are you reading?"

"Hmmm?"

"What are you reading? What's it about?" Finally, once I got her attention, she'd stop and tell me what the whole book was about. More often than not, they were romantic novels, and the climax came when, after several interruptions and misunderstandings, the man and woman finally kissed. Since I've had a lifelong love of stories, I enjoyed these times enormously, and I'd sit spellbound while she went through the entire plot in great detail, her eyes flashing and arms waving. Listening to her stories made me want to learn to read, because then, I figured, I could enjoy stories whenever I wanted.

Mama's brother who lived with us, Uncle Abdullah, had come to London with his sister, so he could attend the university. He asked me if I wanted to go to school. "You know, Waris, you need to learn how to read. If you're interested, I can help you." He told me where the school was located, what times it met— and most important—that it was free. The notion that I could go to school would have never occurred to me on my own. The ambassador paid me a tiny sum each month for pocket money, but certainly not enough to pay for school. Excited about learning to read, I went to Auntie Maruim and told her I wanted to go to school. I wanted to learn how to read, write, and speak English.

Even though I lived in London, we spoke Somali at home, and since I had no contact with the outside world, I knew only a few words of English. Auntie said, "Well, let me think about it." But when she discussed it with my uncle, he said no. I kept pressing her to let me go, but she didn't want to go against my uncle. Finally, I decided to go without their permission. School met three nights a week, from nine to eleven. Uncle Abdullah agreed to take me the first time and show me where to go. By now I was about fifteen, and this was my first time in a classroom ever. The room was full of people of all ages from all over the world. After the first night, an old Italian man would pick me up when I sneaked out of my uncle's house, then bring me home again when we were finished. I was so eager to learn that the teacher would say to me, "You're good, Waris, but slow down." I learned the alphabet, and was beginning on the fundamentals of English, when my uncle discovered I was sneaking out at night. He was furious that I'd disobeyed him and put an end to my attending school after only a couple of weeks.

Even though I was no longer permitted to go to school, I borrowed my cousin's books and tried to teach myself to read. I wasn't allowed to watch TV with the family, but sometimes I'd linger at the door and listen to the English, trying to develop an ear for the language. Everything continued as usual until one day Auntie Maruim called to me as I was cleaning. "Waris, come down here when you've finished upstairs. I have something to tell you." I was making the beds, and when I'd done them all I walked into the living room, where my aunt stood by the fireplace.

"Yes?"

"I got a phone call today from home. Ah . . . what's your little brother's name?"

"Ali?"

"No, the youngest one, the little one with gray hair."

"Old Man? You're talking about Old Man?"

"Yeah. Old Man and your big sister, Aman. Well, I'm sorry. They both died." I couldn't believe what I was hearing. My eyes fixed on Auntie's face, thinking she must be joking—or maybe she was mad at me about something, and she was trying to punish me by telling me that awful story. But she had no expression of any kind to give me a clue; her face was completely blank. *She must be serious, or why would she say this? But how can it be true?* I froze in that spot and couldn't move, until I felt my legs giving way, and sat down on the white sofa for a minute. I didn't even think to ask what had happened. My aunt might have been talking, she might have explained the horrible events to me, but all I could hear was a roaring in my ears. Numbly, walking stiffly like a zombie, I went up to my room on the fourth floor.

I lay there in shock for the rest of the day, stretched out on my bed under the eaves in the tiny room that I shared with my young cousin. Old Man and Aman both dead! How could it be? I had left home, missing my opportunity to spend time with my brother and sister, and now I would never see either one of them again. Aman, always the strong one; Old Man, always the wise one. It didn't seem possible that they could die—and if *they* could, what did that mean for the rest of the family—those of us with lesser abilities?

By that evening, I decided I didn't want to suffer anymore. Nothing in my life had gone the way I'd hoped since that morning I ran away from my father. Now, two years later, I missed the closeness of my family terribly, and knowing two of them were gone forever was more than I could bear. I walked downstairs to the kitchen, opened a drawer, and removed a butcher knife. With the knife in my hand I returned upstairs to my room. But as I lay there trying to get the courage to cut myself, I kept thinking of my mother. Poor Mama. I lost two this week, she'd lose three. It hardly seemed fair to her, so I laid the knife on the table next to the bed and stared at the ceiling. I'd forgotten about the knife, when later my cousin Basma came in to check on me. She looked at it in shock. "What the hell is that! What are you doing with a knife?" I didn't try to answer, just went back to looking at the ceiling. Basma took the knife and went away.

After a few days my aunt called me again: "Waris! Come down." I lay there pretending not to hear. "WARIS! COME DOWN!" I went downstairs and found her waiting at the foot. "Hurry up! Telephone!" This news astonished me, as I never got phone calls. In fact, I'd never spoken on the telephone.

"For me?" I said quietly.

"Yes, yes." She pointed to the receiver lying on the table. "Here, pick it up—pick up the phone!"

I held the receiver in my hand, looking at the contraption as if it were going to bite me. From about a foot away, I whispered, "Yes?"

Aunt Maruim rolled her eyes. "Speak! Speak—talk into the phone!" She turned the receiver right side up and pushed it next to my ear.

"Hello?" Then I heard an amazing sound: my mother's voice. "Mama! Mama! Oh, my God, is it really you?" A grin spread across my face for the first time in days. "Mama, are you okay?"

"No, I've been living under the tree." She told me that after Aman and Old Man died, she went crazy. At this point in Mama's story, I was so thankful I had given up the notion of adding to her grief by killing myself. My mother had run into the desert; she didn't want to be with anyone, look at anyone, talk to anyone. Then she went on to Mogadishu alone and visited her family. She was still there with them now, calling from Auntie Sahru's house.

Mama tried to explain how it happened, but still nothing made sense. Old Man had fallen ill. As was so typical of our lives as nomads in Africa, there was no medical help; nobody knew what was wrong, or what to do about it. In that society there were only two alternatives: live or die. There was no in between. As long as someone lived, everything was okay. We didn't worry much about illness, since without doctors or medicine, there was nothing we could do to fix it. When someone died, well, that was okay, too, because the survivors would continue. Life went on. Always, the philosophy of *in'shallah* ruled our lives: "If God is willing." There was an acceptance of life as a gift, and death as the unarguable decision of God.

But when Old Man fell sick, my parents were frightened, because he was a special child. Mama—not knowing what else to do—had sent a messenger to Aman in Mogadishu, asking for help. Aman was always the strong one; she would know what to do. And she did. Aman set off on foot from Mogadishu to come and get Old Man and take him to a doctor. Exactly where my family was camped at the time, or how far they were from the capital, I have no idea. But what Mama couldn't have known when she sent for her was that Aman was eight months pregnant. As my sister carried Old Man to the hospital, he died in her arms. Aman went into shock, and she also died a few days later, and the baby with her. I was never even sure where they were when they died, but after learning this, Mama, who had always been so quietly steadfast, fell apart. And since she was the center that held our family together, it sickened me to think what life was like for the rest of them. More than ever, I felt terrible about being stuck in London and unable to help Mama when she needed me most.

However, life went on for all of us, and in London I tried to enjoy it as much as I could. I did my duties in the house, and joked with my cousins and their friends who visited.

One night I recruited Basma to help me with my first modeling job. Since arriving in London, I had grown to love clothes, but I didn't particularly want to own them—there was just something fun about trying them on. It was like playacting; I could pretend to be someone else. While the family was in the den watching television, I went into Uncle Mohammed's room and closed the door. I opened his armoire and took out one of his best suits, a navy wool pinstripe. I laid it on the bed with a white shirt, silk tie, dark socks, elegant black English shoes, and felt hat. I put everything on, struggling to knot the tie as I'd seen Uncle do. Then I pulled the hat down low. When my ensemble was complete, I went to find Basma. She doubled over laughing.

"Go tell your dad there's a man here to see him."

"Those are his clothes? Oh, my God, he's going to kill—"

"Just go do it."

I stood out in the hallway and listened to my cousin, waiting for the right moment to make my big entrance. "Father," I heard Basma say, "there's a man here to see you."

"A man at this time of night?" Uncle Mohammed didn't sound too happy. "Who is it? What does he want? Have you ever seen him before?"

Basma stammered, "I, uh, I don't know. I think, yeah, I think you know him."

"Well, tell him . . ."

"Why don't you see him," she said quickly. "He's right outside the door."

"Okay," my uncle agreed tiredly. That was my cue. I pulled the hat all the way down over my eyes till I could barely see, stuck my hands in the pockets of his jacket, and swaggered into the room.

"Hi, don't you remember me?" I said in a baritone voice. Uncle's eyes bugged out, and he ducked down trying to get a look under the hat. When he realized who it was, he cracked up laughing. Auntie and all the rest of the family roared.

Uncle Mohammed wagged his finger at me. "Now, did I give you permission to . . ."

"I just had to try, Uncle. Don't you think it's fun?"

"Oh, Allah."

I did this stunt a few more times, each time waiting long enough till I figured my uncle wasn't expecting it. Then he would say to me, "That's enough, now, Waris. Don't try on my clothes anymore, all right? Leave them alone." And I knew he was serious, but still he thought it was funny. Later I'd hear him laughing and telling his friends, "This girl will go in my room and try on my clothes. Then Basma will come in and say, `Dad, there's a man here to see you.' Then she strolls in wearing my things from head to toe. You should see it. . . ."

My auntie said her friends had mentioned that I should try modeling. But Auntie's response was "Um-hmmm. But we don't do that sort of thing, being from Somalia and being Moslem, you know." However, my aunt never seemed to object to the modeling career of her old friend's daughter, Iman. Auntie had known Iman's mother for years and years, so whenever either of them were in London, Aunt Maruim insisted they stay with us. Listening to discussions of Iman was how I first became acquainted with the idea of modeling. I had cut many of her pictures from my cousin's magazines and taped them to the wall in my little room. If she's a Somali woman and she can do this, I reasoned, why can't I?

When Iman came to our house, I always wanted to find the right opportunity to talk to her. I wanted to ask, "How do I become a model?" I barely even knew that such a thing existed; I certainly had no idea how to become one. But each time she'd visit, she would spend the evening talking with the elders; I knew my aunt and uncle would never approve of my interrupting their conversation for such nonsense as my desire to be a model. Finally, one night I found the right moment. Iman was in her room reading, and I knocked on the door. "Can I get you something before you go to sleep?"

"Yes, I'd like a cup of herbal tea." I went down to the kitchen and brought back a tray.

As I set it down on the nightstand, I began. "You know, I have so many of your pictures in my room." I listened to the clock ticking on the nightstand, feeling like a perfect idiot. "I'd really like to do modeling, too. Do you think it's hard . . . how did you do it . . . how did you start, anyway?"

I don't know what I expected her to say; maybe I hoped she'd wave a magic wand over me and turn me into Cinderella. But my dream of modeling was an abstract one; the whole idea seemed so far-fetched that I didn't spend much time thinking about it. Instead, after that night, I went on with my daily chores, focusing on the day-to-day business of breakfast, lunch, dishes, and dusting.

By this point I was about sixteen, and had lived in London

for two years. I had actually become acclimated enough that I knew what date the Western world attributed to this span of time: 1983.

During the summer of that year, Uncle Mohammed's sister died in Germany, leaving behind a young daughter. Her daughter, little Sophie, came to live with us, and my uncle enrolled her in All Souls Church School. My morning routine now also included walking Sophie several blocks to her school.

On one of those first mornings, as Sophie and I strolled toward the old brick building, I saw a strange man staring at me. He was a white man around forty with a ponytail. He didn't try to hide the fact he was staring at me and, in fact, he was quite bold. After I left Sophie at the door, the man walked toward me and started speaking to me. But of course I didn't speak English, so I had no idea what he was saying. Frightened, I wouldn't look at him and ran back home. This routine continued: I'd drop off Sophie, the white man would be waiting, he'd try to talk to me, and I'd run.

On the walk home after I met Sophie in the afternoons, she'd frequently mention a new friend—a little girl she'd met in her class. "Yeah, um-hmmm," I'd say, completely uninterested. One day I was a little bit late arriving to pick up Sophie. When I got there, she was waiting outside the school, playing with another little girl. "Oh, Waris, this is my friend," Sophie said proudly. Standing next to the two girls was the man with the ponytail, the guy who had been bothering me for nearly a year.

"Yeah, let's go," I said nervously, eyeing my man. But he bent over and said something to Sophie, who spoke English, German, and Somali. "Come on, Sophie. Get away from that man," I warned, and snatched her hand.

She turned to me and said brightly, "He wants to know if you speak English." Sophie shook her head at the man. He said something else and Sophie translated, "He wants to ask you something."

"Tell him I'm not talking to him," I replied haughtily and

looked in the other direction. "He can just go away. He can just . . ." But I decided not to finish my sentence, because his daughter was listening, and Sophie would immediately translate. "Forget it. Let's just go," and I grabbed at her hand and pulled her away.

Shortly after this encounter, I dropped Sophie off one morning as usual. Then I walked back home and was upstairs cleaning when the doorbell rang. I headed downstairs, but before I could reach the door, Aunt Maruim was opening it. Peering through the railing from the stair landing I couldn't believe what I saw; there stood Mr. Ponytail. He must have followed me. My first thought was that he was going to make up some stories to tell my aunt—say that I was doing something wrong. Some lies, like I was flirting with him, slept with him, or he'd caught me stealing something. Auntie said in her fluent English, "Who are you?"

"My name is Malcolm Fairchild. I'm sorry to bother you— but can I talk to you?"

"What do you want to talk to me about?" I could see Auntie was shocked.

Walking back upstairs, I felt ill, wondering what he was going to say, but within two seconds I heard the door slam shut. I rushed into the living room as Aunt Maruim was storming toward the kitchen.

"Auntie, who was that?"

"I don't know—some man who said he's been following you, wanted to talk to you, some nonsense about wanting to take your picture." She glared at me.

"Auntie, I didn't tell him to do it. I didn't say anything to him."

"I KNOW THAT! That's why he's here!" She marched past me. "Go do your work—don't worry about it. I took care of *him*." But Auntie refused to go into details about their conversation, and the fact that she'd been so angry and disgusted led me to believe he wanted to take some sort of porno pictures. I was horrified and never brought up the incident after that morning.

From then on, each time I saw him at All Souls Church School, he never talked to me. He simply smiled politely and went on about his business. Until one day when I was picking up Sophie, he startled me by walking up and handing me a card. My eyes never left his face as I took it and stowed it in my pocket. I watched him steadily as he turned around to walk away, then started cussing him in Somali: "Get away from me, you dirty man—you fucking pig!"

When I got home, I ran upstairs; the kids all slept on the top floors, so this part of the house was our sanctuary from the adults. I went into my cousin's room and, as usual, interrupted her reading. "Basma, look at this," I said, fishing the card from my pocket. "This is from that man, remember that man I told you about, the one who's always bothering me, and who followed me here? He gave me this card today. What does it say?"

"It says he's a photographer."

"But what kind of photographer?"

"He takes pictures."

"Yeah, but what kind of pictures?"

"It says, 'fashion photographer.' "

"Fashion photographer," I said, sounding out each word slowly. "You mean, he takes pictures of clothes? He'd take pictures of me wearing clothes?"

"I don't know, Waris," she sighed. "I really don't know." I knew I was bothering her, that she wanted to get back to her book. Standing up from the bed, I took the card and left. But I hid the fashion photographer's card in my room. Some little voice told me to hang on to it.

My cousin Basma was my only adviser; this girl was always there for me. And never was I more grateful for her guidance than when I sought advice concerning her brother Haji.

Haji was twenty-four years old, my uncle's second-oldest son. He was considered very bright and, like Uncle Abdullah, was attending university in London. Haji had always been friendly to me from the time I arrived in London. When I'd be upstairs cleaning, he'd say, "Hey, Waris, are you finished with the bathroom?"

"No," I'd reply, "but if you want it, go ahead and I'll clean it afterward."

"Oh, no . . . I just wondered if you needed some help." Or he'd say, "I'm going to get something to drink. Would you like something?" I was pleased that my cousin cared for me. We frequently talked and joked around.

Sometimes, when I opened the door to walk out of the bathroom, he was standing right outside, and wouldn't let me pass. When I tried to duck around him, he moved too. When I tried to push him, yelling, "Get out of my way, you slob," he'd laugh. These little games went on, and although I tried to shrug them off as corny jokes, I was confused. There was something underneath his behavior that made me nervous. He'd look at me in a funny, moony-eyed way, or he'd stand a bit too close. When I'd get that queasy feeling, I tried to stop and remind myself, *No, come on, Waris, Haji is like your brother. What you're thinking is sick.*

Then one day I was walking out of the bathroom carrying my cleaning bucket and rags and when I opened the door he was standing there. He grabbed my arm and pushed himself against me, his face a hair's width from mine. "What's going on here?" I started laughing nervously.

"Oh—nothing, nothing." He turned me loose instantly. I took my bucket and went to the next room, very casually, as if nothing had happened. But my mind was racing, and after that moment, I didn't wonder anymore if something was going on. I knew. I knew something wasn't healthy here.

The next night I was in my room asleep, and my cousin Shukree, Basma's little sister, was asleep in her bed. But I'm a very light sleeper, and around three in the morning, I heard someone coming up the stairs; I figured it must be Haji, since his room was across the hall from mine. He'd just gotten home, and from the way he was stumbling in the hallway, I could tell he was drunk. This sort of behavior was not tolerated in my uncle's household—coming in at this hour, and certainly nobody drank. They were strict Moslems, and drinking alcohol of any kind was forbidden. But I guess Haji thought he was old enough to be his own man and he'd give it a try.

The door to my room opened quietly and my body went rigid. Both the beds in this room were on a raised platform, up a couple of steps from the door. I could see Haji tiptoeing up the stairs, trying hard not to wake my little cousin, who was in the bed closest to the door. But he missed a step and tripped, then crawled the rest of the way over to my bed. In the light from the windows behind him, I watched him craning his neck to see my face in the shadows. "Hey, Waris," he whispered. "Waris . . ." His breath reeked of liquor, confirming my suspicion that he must be drunk. But I lay completely still in the darkness, pretending to be asleep. He reached out his hand and started feeling around the pillow to find my face. I thought, *Oh, my God, please don't let this happen.* Snorting, "HAYYUH," I flopped over on my side as if I were dreaming, trying to make enough noise to wake up Shukree. At this point he lost his nerve and ran quietly back to his room.

The next day I went to Basma's room. "Look, I need to talk to you." I guess the look of panic on my face told her this wasn't one of my ordinary visits just to kill time.

"Come in, close the door."

"This is about your brother," I said, taking a deep breath. I didn't know how to tell her this, and I just prayed she'd believe me.

"What about him?" Now she looked alarmed.

"Last night he came into my room. It was three o'clock in the morning and pitch-black."

"What did he do?"

"He was trying to touch my face. He whispered my name."

"Oh, no. Are you sure? You weren't dreaming?"

"Come on. I see the way he looks at me, the way he looks at me when I'm alone with him. I don't know what to do."

"Shit—SHIT! Get a fucking cricket bat and put it under your bed. Or a broom. No—take the rolling pin from the kitchen. Put that under your bed, and when he comes into your room at night, mash him in the head! And you know what else to do?" she added. "Scream. Scream your head off so everybody can hear." Thank God, this girl was definitely on my side.

All day I kept praying, "Please don't make me do this horrible thing; please just make him stop." I didn't want to make trouble. I worried about what lies he might offer his parents as an explanation, or that they might throw me out. I just wanted him to stop—no more games, no more late-night visits, no more groping—because I had a sick feeling where it was all headed. But my instincts told me to prepare for battle in case prayer didn't work.

That night I went to the kitchen, smuggled the rolling pin up to my room, and hid it under the bed. Later, when my cousin was asleep, I brought it out and laid it next to me, never releasing my grip on the handle. And in a repeat performance of the previous night, Haji came in around three in the morning. He paused in the doorway and I saw the light from the hallway glinting off his glasses. I lay there with one eye open, watching him. He crept over to my pillow and started tapping me on the arm. His breath stank of Scotch so bad that I wanted to gag, but I didn't move an inch. Then, kneeling next to the bed, Haji groped around until he found the bottom hem of the covers, and pushed his hand underneath and across the mattress to my leg. Sliding his palm up my thigh, he was going all the way to my knickers, my underwear.

I have to break his glasses, I thought, *so at least there's proof he was in the room.* I tightened my hand around the rolling-pin handle and brought the wood down across his face with all my might. First there was a sickening thud, then I screamed, "GET OUT OF MY FUCKIN' ROOM, YOU FUCKIN'—"

Shukree sat up in her bed, crying, "What's happening?" Within seconds I heard footsteps running from all corners of the house. But because I had broken Haji's glasses, he couldn't see, so he resorted to crawling back to his room on hands and knees. He got into his bed with all his clothes on, pretending to be asleep.

Basma came in and threw on the lights. Of course she was in on the whole plan but pretended total ignorance. "What's going on here?"

Shukree explained: "Haji was in here, crawling around on the floor!"

When Aunt Maruim walked in with her robe pulled around her, I yelled, "Auntie, he was in my room! He was in my room, and he did it yesterday too! And I hit him!" I pointed at Haji's shattered glasses next to my bed.

"Shhh," she said sternly. "I don't want to hear this—not now. Everybody, get back to your rooms. Go to bed."

10.

FREE AT LAST

After the night I mashed Haji's face with the rolling pin, no one in the house ever mentioned the incident again. I might have thought his late-night visits were merely a bad dream, except for one big difference. Whenever I saw Haji in the hallway, he no longer gazed at me with longing. That expression had been replaced by one of naked hatred. I was thankful that as I'd prayed, this unpleasant chapter in my life had come to an end. However, it was soon replaced by a new concern.

Uncle Mohammed announced that in a few weeks the family would be returning to Somalia. His four-year term as Somalian ambassador was up, and we were going home. Four years had sounded like a lifetime to me when I'd first arrived, but now I couldn't believe the time was over. Unfortunately, I wasn't excited about going back to Somalia. I wanted to go home wealthy and successful, as every African dreams of returning home from a rich nation like England. In a poor country like my homeland, people are constantly searching for a way out, clawing to make it to Saudi or Europe or the States, so they can make some money to help their destitute families.

Now here I was about to return home after four years abroad—with nothing. What could I say I'd accomplished when I went back? Would I tell my mother I'd learned how to cook pasta? Back traveling with my camels, I'd probably never see pasta again. Would I tell my father I'd learned how to scrub toilets? "Huh? What's a toilet?" he'd say. Ah, but money, *cash*, there was something he could understand—the universal language. There was something my family had never had much of.

By the time my aunt and uncle were ready to return to Somalia, I had saved a pittance from my maid's wages, which was difficult enough considering my pathetic salary. My dream, however, was to make enough money to buy my mother a house—a place where Mama could live without having to travel constantly and work so hard to survive. This isn't as far-fetched as it might sound, since with the exchange rate, I could buy a house in Somalia for a couple of thousand dollars. To accomplish this goal, I felt since I was already in England, I wanted to stay and make some money, because once I left, I certainly couldn't come back. How I would manage this, I didn't know. But I had faith that somehow things would work out, once I was free from working like a slave for my aunt and uncle. However, they didn't agree. "What on earth are you going to do here?" my aunt exclaimed. "An eighteen-year-old girl, with no place to stay, no money, no job, no work permit, and no English? It's ridiculous! You're coming home with us."

Long before the scheduled departure, Uncle Mohammed advised us all of two things: the date we were leaving, and the need to make sure our passports were in order. I did. I promptly took mine into the kitchen, sealed it in a plastic bag, then buried it in the garden.

Waiting till the day before our flight to Mogadishu, I announced that I couldn't find my passport. My plan was simple enough: if I didn't have a passport, they couldn't take me back. Uncle smelled something rotten and kept asking, "Well, Waris, where could your passport be? Where have you been that you could possibly have left it?" Obviously he knew the answer to that question, since in four years I had barely been out of the house.

"I don't know—maybe I accidentally threw it away while I was cleaning," I answered with a straight face. He was still the ambassador and he could help me if he wanted. I kept hoping that if my uncle realized how desperately I wanted to stay, he wouldn't make me go home, but instead would help me get a visa.

"Well, *now* what are we going to do, Waris? We can't just leave you here!" He was livid that I'd put him in this position. For the next twenty-four hours we played a game of nerves, to see who would give in. I kept insisting my passport was lost; Uncle Mohammed kept insisting there was nothing he could do to help me.

Aunt Maruim had her own ideas. "We'll just tie you up, put you in a bag, and smuggle you on board the plane! People do it all the time."

This threat got my attention. "If you do that," I said slowly, "I'll never, ever, forgive you. Look, Auntie, just leave me here. I'll be fine."

"Yeah, yeah, you'll be fine," she answered sarcastically. "NO, you are NOT going to be fine." I could see in her face that she was very worried, but was she worried enough to help me? She had plenty of friends in London; my uncle had all his contacts at the embassy. A simple phone call was all it would take to provide me with a link to survival, but I knew if they believed for an instant they could bluff me into coming back to Somalia, they wouldn't make that call.

The next morning the entire four-story mansion was in complete chaos with everyone packing, the phone ringing, and swarms of people running in and out of the house. Upstairs, I prepared to leave my little room under the eaves, packing my cheap bag with what few belongings I'd accumulated during my stay in England. In the end, I threw most of the hand-me-down clothes in the trash, deciding they were too ugly and old-womanish for me. Why haul around a bunch of garbage? Still a nomad, I'd travel light.

At eleven o'clock, everyone gathered in the living room as the chauffeur loaded the bags into the car. I paused for a second to remember this was the way I had come so many years ago—the chauffeur, the car, walking into this room, seeing the white sofa, the fireplace, meeting my aunt for the first time. That gray morning was also the first time I'd seen snow. Everything about this country had seemed so bizarre to me then. I walked outside to the car with my distressed Aunt Maruim, who said, "What am I going to tell your mother?"

"Tell her I'm fine, and she'll hear from me soon." She shook her head and got into the car. I stood on the sidewalk and waved good-bye to everyone, then walked into the street, watching the car until it was out of sight.

I'm not going to lie—I was scared. Up until that moment I hadn't really believed that they would leave me there all alone. But as I stood in the middle of Harley Street, I was exactly that—all alone. I have no hard feelings toward my aunt and uncle, though; they're still my family. They gave me an opportunity by bringing me to London, and for that I will forever be grateful. When they left, I guess they thought, "Well, you wanted to stay—here's your chance. Go ahead then—do what you want. But we're not going to make it easy for you, because we think you should come home with us." I'm sure they felt it was a disgrace for a young woman to remain in England alone, unchaperoned. However, in the end the decision had been mine, and since I had chosen to remain, I would have to take charge of my own destiny now.

Fighting an overwhelming feeling of panic, I went back

inside the house. I closed the front door and walked into the kitchen to talk to the only other person left—my old friend the chef. He greeted me with "Well, you know, you've got to go today. I'm the only one who's staying on—not you. You've got to leave." He pointed toward the front door. Oh, yes, the minute my uncle was gone, he just couldn't wait to give it to me. The smug look on his unfriendly face showed that ordering me around gave him great pleasure. I stood there leaning against the door frame, thinking how quiet the house seemed now that everybody was gone. "Waris, you've got to go now. I want you to get out . . ."

"Oh, *shut up*." The man was like an obnoxious barking dog. "I'm going, okay? I just came in to get my bag."

"Grab it now—quickly. Quickly. Hurry up, because I have to—" By this time I was climbing the stairs, paying no attention to his noise. The master was gone, and in the brief interim before the new ambassador arrived, Chef would be master. I walked through the empty rooms, thinking of all the good and bad times here, wondering where my next home would be.

I picked up my little duffel from the bed, slung it over my shoulder, walked down the four flights of stairs, and out the front door. Unlike the day I had arrived, today was a gorgeous, sunny day with a blue sky and fresh air like springtime. In the tiny garden, I used a stone to unearth my passport, slipping it out of its plastic bag and stowing it in my duffel. I brushed the soil from my hands and headed down the street. I couldn't help smiling as I walked along the sidewalk—free at last. My whole life stretched before me with nowhere to go, and no one to answer to. And somehow I knew things would work out.

Close to my uncle's house was my first stop: the Somalian embassy. I knocked on the door. The doorman who answered knew my family well, since sometimes he also drove for my uncle. "Hello, miss. What are you doing here? Is Mr. Farah still in town?"

"No, he's gone. I wanted to see Anna, to find out if I can get a job at the embassy." He laughed, returned to his chair, and sat down. He put his hands behind his head and leaned back against the wall. As I stood there in the middle of the lobby, he made no attempt to move. His attitude puzzled me, as this man had always been polite to me. Then I realized that—like Chef's—his attitude had changed with the departures that occurred that morning. My uncle was gone, and without my uncle, I was nobody. I was less than nobody, and these oafs were thrilled to have the upper hand.

"Oh! Anna's far too busy to see you." The doorman grinned.

"Look," I said firmly, "*I need to see her.*" Anna had been my uncle's secretary, and she'd always been kind to me. Luckily, she heard my voice in the lobby and walked out of her office to see what was happening.

"Waris! What are you doing here?"

"You know, I really didn't want to go back to Somalia with my uncle," I explained. "I just didn't want to go back. So I—I'm not staying at the house anymore, you know. And I was wondering if you know anybody who maybe—anybody I can work for—anything—I don't care what it is. I'll do anything."

"Well, my darling"—she raised her eyebrows—"it's a bit too short notice. Where are you staying?"

"Oh, I don't know. Don't worry about that."

"Well, can you give me a number where I can find you?"

"No, because I don't know where I'm staying. I'll find some cheap hotel tonight." I knew she would invite me to stay at her place if she hadn't had a tiny little flat. "But I can come back and give you a number later, so you can let me know if you hear of anything."

"Okay, Waris. Listen, take care of yourself—are you sure you're going to be all right?"

"Yeah, I'll be fine." From the corner of my eye I saw the doorman constantly grinning like a fool. "Well, thanks—look, I'll see you later."

Above: Waris on a photo shoot in Mali, Africa, 1994 *Below:* Waris and her mother reunited in Galadi, Ethiopia (near the Somali border), 1995

Photograph by Gerry Pomeroy

Waris on a photo shoot in the British Virgin Islands, 1995

Above: Waris and Herb
Ritts on a photo shoot in
the Arizona desert, 1995

Below: Waris on a photo
shoot in the
Mexican jungle, 1996

Above left: Waris on holiday in Gabon, Africa, 1996 *Above right:* Waris and Dana on holiday in Gabon, 1996 *Below:* Dana and Aleeke at home in Brooklyn, January 1998

Right: Waris on holiday on St. John in the Virgin Islands, Christmas, 1997

Below: Waris as photographed by Koto Bolofo for Italian *Marie Claire,* spring 1997 *Courtesy of Italian Marie Claire*

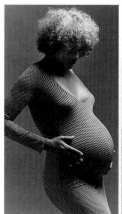

Waris nine months pregnant with son Aleeke
Photographs by Sharon Schuster

Waris on trip to London on behalf of the United Nations, spring 1998
Photograph by Harry Borden/IPG

With relief I headed out into the sunlight again, and decided to go shopping. All I had to live on until I landed a job was the small sum of money I'd squirreled away from my maid's wages. But now that I was a woman about town, I needed to buy something decent to wear, a new dress to lift my spirits. I walked from the embassy to the big department stores at Oxford Circus. I'd been there before with my cousin Basma when I'd first come to London. Aunt Maruim had sent us down to buy me a few things, since when I arrived I had no winter clothes. Actually I'd had no clothes at all, except the outfit I'd worn on the plane and one fine leather sandal.

Strolling through the racks at Selfridges, I found the enormous variety of choices mesmerizing. The thought that I could stay here as long as I wanted and try on all these clothes—all these colors, styles, sizes—was intoxicating. The thought that for the first time in my history, I was in charge of my own life was intoxicating—nobody yelling at me to milk the goats, feed the babies, make the tea, scrub the floors, scour the toilets.

For the next several hours, I set to work trying on outfits in the dressing room with the help of two sales clerks. Using my limited English and sign language, I communicated that I wanted something longer, shorter, tighter, brighter. At the end of my marathon session, when dozens of discarded garments lay in stacks outside my fitting room, one of the clerks smiled at me and said, "Well, love, what did you decide to have?"

The sheer volume of choices overwhelmed me, but by this point I was getting nervous that down the street, in the next store, there might be something even better. Before I parted with any of my precious pounds, I'd better find out. "I'm not having anything today," I said pleasantly, "but thank you." The poor clerks, standing with their arms full of dresses, looked at me in disbelief, then at each other in disgust. I sailed past them and continued on my mission: to examine every inch of Oxford Street.

After several places, I still hadn't bought anything; but as always, the true joy for me was simply to try on things. As I left one building and entered another, I realized the spring-like day was fading, the winter evening coming on, and I still had no place to spend the night. With this thought in mind, I entered the next store and saw a tall, attractive African woman examining a sale table of sweaters. She looked like a Somalian, and I studied her, trying to decide how to talk to her. Picking up a sweater, I smiled at her and said in Somali, "I'm trying to buy something, but I can't decide what I want. And believe me, girl, I've seen a lot of clothes today."

We began talking and the woman said her name was Halwu. She was quite friendly and laughed a lot. "Where do you live, Waris? What do you do?"

"Oh, you're going to laugh. I'm sure you'll think I'm crazy, but I live nowhere. I don't have any place to live, because my family left me today. They went back to Somalia." I saw the look of empathy in her eyes; as I later learned this woman had been through a lot herself.

"You didn't want to go back to Somalia, huh?" Without saying it, we both knew: we missed our home and our families, but what opportunities did we have there? Being traded for camels? Becoming some man's property? Struggling every day just to survive?

"No, but I have nothing here, either," I said. "My uncle was the ambassador, but now he's gone and the new man is coming. So this morning they kicked me out, and right this minute, I have no idea where I'm headed." I laughed.

She waved in the air to silence me, as if the movement of her hand could sweep away all my problems. "Look, I live around the corner at the YMCA. I don't have a big place, but you can come and stay for the night. I just have a room, so if you want to cook, you'll have to go to a different floor to make some food."

"Ooohh, that would be wonderful, but are you sure?"

"Yes, I'm sure. I mean, come on. What are you going to do otherwise?"

We walked together to her room at the Y. The YMCA was located in a modern brick high-rise normally occupied by students. Her room was a tiny space with a twin bed, a place for books, and Halwu's big, beautiful television. "Oh!" I threw up my hands. "Can I watch TV?"

The woman looked at me like I was from outer space. "Oh, yeah—sure. Switch it on." I plopped down on the floor in front of it and stared greedily at her TV. After four years, I could look at it without somebody chasing me out of the room like a stray cat. "Didn't you ever watch television at your uncle's?" she said curiously.

"Are you kidding? Sometimes I would sneak in, but I'd always get caught. `Watching TV again, Waris?' " I mimicked my aunt's snottiest voice and started snapping my fingers. " 'Back to work, now, come on. We didn't bring you here to watch television.' "

My real education on life in London began with Halwu as my professor; the two of us became close friends. I spent that first night in her room, and the next, and the next. Then she suggested, "Why don't you get a room here?"

"Well, first of all because I can't afford it, and I need to go to school, which means I won't have time to work." I asked her shyly, "Can you read and write?"

"Yeah."

"And speak English?"

"Yeah."

"See, I can't do any of those things and I need to learn. That's my biggest priority. And if I start working again, I won't have time."

"Well, why don't you go to school part-time and work

part-time? Don't worry about what kind of job it is—just take anything until you learn English."

"Will you help me?"

"Sure, I'll help you."

I tried to get a room at the YMCA, but it was full with a waiting list. All the young people wanted to be there because it was cheap and very social, with an Olympic-size pool and fitness center. I added my name to the list, but in the meantime I knew I had to do something because I couldn't keep taking up poor Halwu's space. Right across from the YMCA, however, was the YWCA; it was full of elderly people, and fairly depressing, but I took a room there temporarily and set out to find a job. My friend suggested logically, "Why don't you start by looking right here?"

"What do you mean? Right where?"

"Right here. Right here," she said, pointing. "McDonald's is just next door."

"I can't work there—there's no way I can serve people. Don't forget, I can't speak English or read. Besides, I don't have a work permit." But Halwu knew the ropes, and following her suggestion, I went around back and applied for a job cleaning the kitchen.

When I began working for McDonald's, I found out how right she was. I thought that for the hard work I did the wages were poor and that perhaps the management took advantage of my illegal status. As long as you were a hard worker, the management didn't care about your story.

My career as kitchen help at McDonald's put to use the skills I'd learned as a maid: I washed dishes, wiped counters, scrubbed grills, and mopped floors, in a constant effort to erase the traces of burger grease. When I went home at night I was coated with grease and stank like grease. In the kitchen we were always short-staffed, but I didn't dare complain. None of that mattered because, at least now I could support myself. I was just grateful to have the job, and besides, I knew I wouldn't be there for long. In the meantime, I'd do whatever it took to survive.

I began going part-time to the foreigners' free language school, improving my English and learning how to read and write. But for the first time in years, my life wasn't only about work. Sometimes Halwu took me to nightclubs, where the whole crowd seemed to know her. She talked, laughed, and was hysterically funny—just generally so lively that everybody wanted to be around her. One night we went out and had been dancing for hours until I suddenly looked up to realize we were surrounded by men. "Damn!" I whispered to my friend. "Do these men like us?"

She grinned. "Oh, *yeah*. They like us very much." This notion astonished me. I scanned their faces and decided she was right. I had never had a boyfriend, or even the attention of any male other than my cousin Haji—which hadn't exactly flattered me. For the past four years I'd simply considered myself Miss Nobody—the maid. Now here were these guys lining up to dance with us. I thought, *Waris, girl, you have finally arrived!*

Oddly enough, even though I always liked the black men, it was the white guys who were most interested in me. Overcoming my strict African upbringing, I chatted away, forcing myself to talk with everyone—black, white, male, female. If I was going to be on my own, I reasoned, I had to learn survival skills for this new world, which were different from the ones I was raised with in the desert. Here I needed to learn English, and how to communicate with all sorts of people. Knowing about camels and goats wasn't going to keep me alive in London.

Halwu supplemented these nocturnal nightclub lessons with further instruction the next day. She went through the entire roster of characters we'd met the night before, explaining their motives, their personalities—basically giving me a crash course in human nature. She talked about sex, what these guys were up to, what to watch out for, and the special problems in store for African women like us. Nobody had ever discussed this topic with me in my life. "Have a good time talking, laughing, and dancing with these guys, Waris, then go home. Don't let them talk you into having sex. They don't know that you're different from an English woman; they don't understand that you've been circumcised."

After several months of waiting to get a room at the YMCA, I learned of a woman who wanted to share a room there. She was a student and couldn't afford the room by herself. This was perfect for me, because I couldn't either, and the room was large enough for the two of us. Halwu was a great friend, and I made others at the Y, because the whole place was swarming with young people. I was still going to school, gradually learning English, and working at my McDonald's job. My life was moving along, smooth and steady, but I had no idea how dramatically it was about to change.

One afternoon, I got off work at McDonald's and, still covered with grease, decided to leave through the front, passing by the counter where the customers ordered their food. And there, waiting for a Big Mac, was the man from All Souls Church School and his little girl. "Hello," I said, gliding by.

"Hey, it's you!" Clearly I was the last person he was expecting to see at McDonald's. "How are you?" he said eagerly.

"Fine, fine." To Sophie's friend I said, "And how are you?" I enjoyed showing off my English.

"She's fine," her father replied.

"She's growing quickly, isn't she? Well, I've got to dash. Byebye."

"Wait—where do you live?"

"Bye-bye," I said with a smile. I didn't want to talk to him anymore, because I still didn't trust this guy. The next thing I knew, he'd show up outside my door.

When I got back to the Y, I decided to consult the all-knowing Halwu about this mystery man. I grabbed my passport from the drawer, flipped through its pages, and pulled out Malcolm Fairchild's card from the spot where I'd stuck it the day I buried the little plastic bag in Uncle's garden.

Marching downstairs to Halwu's room, I said, "Tell me something. I have this card, and I've had it a long time. What is this man? I know it says fashion photographer, but what does that mean?"

My friend took the card from my hand. "It means somebody wants to put clothes on you and take your picture."

"You know, I'd really like to do that."

"Who is this man? Where'd you get this card?"

"Oh, he's this guy I met, but I don't really trust him. He gave me his card, then followed me home one day and started saying something to my aunt. She just got pissed off and started yelling at him. But I never really understood what he wanted."

"Well, why don't you call and ask him?"

"You *sure*?" I said, making a face. "Should I? Hey, why don't you come with me and you can talk to him—find out what's the story. My English is still not very good."

"Yeah, go call him."

It took me until the next day before I worked up the courage. As Halwu and I walked down to the pay phone together, my heart pounded a drumbeat in my ears. She put a coin in the slot, and I listened to it click. She held his card in one hand, squinting at it in the dim light of the dark hallway as she dialed. Then a pause. "Yes, may I speak to Malcolm Fairchild?" After exchanging a few opening comments, she got right to the heart of the matter: "You're not some kind of pervert or something, are you? You're not trying to kill my friend? . . . Yeah, but I mean we don't know anything about you—where you live or nothing . . . uh-huh, uh-huh . . . yeah." Halwu was scribbling something on a scrap of paper, and I strained to see over her shoulder.

"What's he saying?" I hissed. She waved at me to be quiet.

"Okay, then. Fair enough . . . we'll do that."

Halwu hung up the phone and took a big breath. "Well, he said, 'Why don't you both come by my studio, and see where I work, if you don't trust me? If you don't want to—well, that's okay, too.'"

I covered my mouth with both fists. "Yes. And? Are we going to go?"

"Shit, yeah, girl. We might as well check it out. Let's find out who this guy is that's been following you around."

11.

THE MODEL

The next day Halwu and I went down to inspect Malcolm Fairchild's studio. I had no idea what to expect, but when we opened the door, I stumbled into another world. Hanging everywhere were enormous posters and billboards featuring pictures of beautiful women. "Oh . . ." I said quietly, spinning around the room, looking at their elegant faces. And I just knew, like I'd known the day when I first heard Uncle Mohammed telling Auntie Sahru back in Mogadishu that he needed a girl to take to London—*this is it*. This is my opportunity—this is where I belong—this is what I want to do.

Malcolm came out and said hello; he told us to relax and gave us a cup of tea. When he sat down, he said to Halwu, "I just want you to know that all I want to do is take her picture." He pointed at me. "I've been following this little girl for over two years, and never have I had such a hard time just to take a photograph."

I stared at him with my mouth hanging open. "That's it?

That's it—you just want to take my picture—a picture like this?" I waved at the posters.

"Yes," he nodded emphatically. "Believe me. That's it." With his hand he drew a line down the center of his nose. "I just want this half of your face"—he turned to Halwu—"because she has the most beautiful profile."

I sat there thinking: All that time wasted! He followed me for two years and it took him two seconds to tell me he just wants to take my picture. "Well, I don't mind doing *that*." But suddenly I became wary, remembering some of my past experiences alone with men. "But she's got to be here, too!" I put my hand on my friend's arm and she nodded. "She's got to be here when you take the picture."

He looked at me with an expression of bafflement. "Yeah, okay. She can come too . . ." By this point I was so excited I was barely touching the chair. "Come day after tomorrow, ten o'clock, and I'll have someone here to do your makeup."

Two days later we returned to his studio. The makeup woman sat me down in a chair and started to work, coming at me with cotton, brushes, sponges, creams, paints, powders, poking me with her fingers, and pulling my skin. I had no idea what she was doing but sat quietly all the same, watching her perform these strange maneuvers with these strange materials. Halwu leaned back in her chair, grinning. Occasionally I would look at her and shrug or make a face. "Be still," the makeup woman commanded.

"Now'—she stepped back and put one hand on her hip and looked at me with satisfaction—"look in the mirror." I stood up and stared in the glass; one side of my face was transformed, all golden, silky, and light with makeup. The other side was plain old Waris.

"Wow! Look at me! But why did you just do one side?" I said in alarm.

"Because he only wants to photograph one side."

"Oh . . ."

She led me out to the studio where Malcolm positioned me on a stool. I swiveled around, studying the dark room full of objects I'd never seen before: the view camera, the lights, the battery packs, the cords hanging everywhere like snakes. He twisted me in front of the camera till I was at a ninety-degree angle to the lens. "Okay, Waris. Put your lips together and stare straight ahead. Chin up. That's it . . . beautiful—" Then I heard a click, followed by a loud pop which made me jump. The flashes went off, the lights blazing for a split second. Somehow, the lights popping made me feel like a different person; suddenly in that moment I imagined myself as one of the movie stars I had seen on the television, smiling into the cameras as they exited their limos at the premieres. Next, he took a piece of paper from the camera and sat looking at his watch.

"What are you doing?" I asked.

"Timing it." Malcolm motioned for me to walk over into the light and pulled off the top layer of paper. As I watched, a woman gradually emerged from the sheet of film as if by magic. When he handed me the Polaroid, I barely recognized myself; the shot showed the right side of my face, but instead of looking like Waris the maid, I looked like Waris the model. They had transformed me into a glamorous creature like the ones posing in Malcolm Fairchild's lobby.

Later in the week, after Malcolm had the film developed, he showed me the finished product. He put the transparencies up on a light box, and I loved them. I asked if he could make more pictures for me. He said it was too expensive, and unfortunately he couldn't afford it. But what he could do was have prints made for me of the shot he'd already taken.

A couple of months after Malcolm had taken my picture, he called me at the Y. "Look, I don't know if you're interested in modeling, but there's some people who want to meet you. One of the modeling agencies saw your photo in my book and said you should call them. If you like, you can sign with their firm and they'll get you jobs."

"Okay . . . but you have to take me there . . . because, you know, I don't feel comfortable going alone. Will you take me there and introduce me?"

"No, I can't do that, but I'll give you the address," he offered.

I carefully chose the ensemble I would wear for my important meeting with Crawford's modeling agency. As it was summer-time, and hot, I put on a red V-necked dress with short sleeves. The dress was not short, not long, but hit me squarely in the middle of the leg and was god-awful ugly.

I walked into the agency wearing my cheap red dress and white sneakers, and thinking: *This is it. I'm happening!* In reality I looked like shit. But even though I cringe whenever I think back to that day, it's just as well that I didn't realize how wrong I looked, because I was still wearing my best outfit. I certainly didn't have the money to go out and buy a new one.

When I arrived the receptionist asked if I had any pictures and I said I had one. She introduced me to a classically beautiful woman, elegantly dressed, named Veronica. Veronica called me into her office and motioned for me to sit down opposite her desk. "How old are you, Waris?"

"I'm young!" These were the first words that came to mind and I blurted them out. "Really—I'm young. These wrinkles' —I pointed to my eyes—"I was born with them."

She gave me a smile. "It's all right." Veronica began writing down my answers, filling out forms. "Where do you live?"

"Oh, I live in Y."

"What, now . . ." She frowned. "Where do you live?"

"I live in YMCA."

"Do you work?"

"Yes."

"What do you do?"

"McDonald's."

"Okay . . . Do you know about modeling?"

"Yes."

"What do you know about it—do you know much?"

"No. I know I want to do it." I repeated this last phrase several times for emphasis.

"Okay. Do you have a book—pictures?"

"No."

"Do you have any family here?"

"No."

"Where is your family?"

"Africa."

"Is that where you're from?"

"Yes, Somalia."

"Okay, so no one here."

"No, none my family here."

"Well. There's a casting right this minute and you have to go."

I was really struggling to understand her, and paused for a minute trying to decipher what she meant by her last statement. "I don't understand, sorry."

"A c-a-s-t-i-n-g." She drew out the word slowly.

"What's casting?"

"You know, it's an interview—when you go for a job and they interview you? Okay? Interview? You understand?"

"Yeah, yeah." I was lying by then. I had no idea what she was talking about. She gave me the address and told me to go straight over.

"I'll call them and tell them you're on your way. Do you have money for a taxi?"

"No, I can walk."

"No, no—it's too far. *Too far*. You have to take a taxi. *Taxi.* Okay? Look, here's ten pounds. Call me when you're finished. Okay?"

———

Riding crosstown in the taxi, I was in complete euphoria. *Oh, oh, oh, I am on my way now.* I'm going to be a model. Then I realized I forgot one thing: I didn't ask her what the job was. *Oh, well, it doesn't matter. I'll be fine because I am one good-looking bitch!*

When I arrived at the casting, I walked into another photographer's studio. I opened the door to a place crawling with professional models—room after room packed full of women with legs up to their necks. They strutted around like lionesses circling for the kill, preening in front of mirrors, bending at the waist to shake their hair, smearing makeup on their legs to make them look dark. I flopped down and said hello to one of the girls sitting next to me. "Um, what is the job?"

"Pirelli calendar."

"Mmmm." I nodded my head wisely. "Prulli calendar. Thank you." *What the hell is that—Prulli calendar?* I was a complete nervous wreck, unable to sit still, crossing and uncrossing my legs, twisting around in my chair until an assistant came out and told me I was next. Then I froze for a minute.

Turning to the girl beside me, I shooed her toward the assistant. "You go. I'm waiting for my friend." I repeated this move each time the assistant came out, until the entire place was empty. Everyone had gone home.

Finally the woman came out, leaned tiredly up against the wall and said, "Come on. You can go now." I stared at her for a minute and I said to myself, *Enough now, Waris. Are you going to do this thing or not? Come on, get up, let's go.*

I followed the woman into the studio and a man with his head glued to the back of a camera yelled out, "Over there. There's the mark." He motioned with one hand.

"Mark?"

"Yeah, stand on the mark."

"Oh, okay. Stand here."

"Okay. Take off your top."

I thought, *Surely I'm not hearing this man right*, but by now I felt ready to vomit. "My top, you mean my shirt?"

He brought his head out from under the drape, and stared at me like I was an idiot. With great irritation he said, "Yeah. Take off your shirt, you know, *why you're here?*"

"But I don't have a bra."

"That's the idea, so we can see your breasts."

"NO!" *What is this shit—my breasts!* Besides, I wasn't wearing a top. All I had on was my red dress. *What does this jerk think I'm going to do, just whip it off and stand there in my fucking underpants and tennis shoes?*

"No. No? Everybody's dying to come to this casting, and you're telling me no?"

"No, no, I'm sorry. Mistake, mistake. I make mistake," and in a panic I headed for the door. When I passed a series of Polaroids scattered across the floor, I bent down to examine them.

The photographer looked at me for a few seconds with his mouth open. Then he turned and called over his shoulder, "Oh, Lord, have we got something in here! Terence, we've got a little problem."

A heavy, robust man with thick gray hair and rosy jowls walked into the room and looked at me curiously. He smiled slightly. "Ah, yes. So what do we have here?"

I stood up straight and tears came to my eyes. "No. That's nothing I can do. I don't do this." I pointed at a photo of a woman nude from the waist up. At first I was simply disappointed. There went my big excitement, my big dream of being a model. *The first job I get and they want me to take my clothes off!* Then I became angry—furious—and I started to cuss them all in Somali. "You dirty fucking men! You shit! You pigs! Keep your fucking job!"

"What are you saying? Look, I'm far too busy for this now—" but by this time I was running out the door, slamming it nearly off the hinges. I cried all the way back to the Y, saying to myself, *I knew there was something sad, something deeply disgusting, about this whole modeling business.*

That evening I was lying on my bed, limp with misery, and my roommate said, "Waris, phone for you."

It was Veronica from the modeling agency. "It's you!" I yelled. "I don't want to talk to you people! You—you embars—embress—" I was trying to pronounce *embarrassed* but I couldn't even choke out that word. "It was terrible. It was very bad; I don't want to do this. I don't want to do this. I don't want to be with you no more!"

"Okay, now calm down, Waris. Do you know who that was today, the photographer?"

"No."

"Do you know who Terence Donovan is?"

"No."

"Well, do you have a friend who speaks English?"

"Yes."

"Well, anybody who speaks English will know who that man is. When we get off the phone, you ask them. He takes pictures of the royal family, Princess Di, and all the big name models. Anyway, he wants to see you again, he's interested in photographing you."

"He asked me to take my clothes off! You didn't tell me that before I went!"

"I know—well, we were in a big hurry; I just thought you were perfect for the job. I explained to him that you couldn't speak English and this sort of thing was against your culture. But this is the Pirelli calendar, and after this job comes out you will get much more work. Do you ever buy the fashion magazines, like *Vogue* and *Elle*?"

"No, I can't afford them. I look at them at the newsstand, but I always put them back."

"Okay, but you've seen them? That's the type of work you're

going to be doing. Terence Donovan is the best; if you want to be a model, you need this job. After this you'll be making all kinds of money, and do whatever you want."

"I'm not taking off my top."

I heard her sigh. "Waris, where did you say you work?"

"McDonald's."

"How much do they pay you?"

I told her.

"Well, he's paying you fifteen hundred pounds for one day."

"All for me? All mine?"

"Yes, and you get to travel, too. The job's in Bath; I don't know if you've been there, but it's a beautiful place. You'll be staying at the Royalton," she added, like I knew what that meant. "Look, do you want to do it, or not?"

By this point she had convinced me. Making this kind of money, I could quickly earn enough to help my mother. "Okay, okay! When can I go back to him?"

"How about tomorrow morning?"

"And I just have to take my top off—that's it? I mean, are you sure for fifteen hundred pounds I don't have to sleep with this man?"

"No, no. It's no trick. Nothing like that."

"Or . . . you know, like he wants me to spread my legs or some shit? If so, tell me now."

"Only take your top off. But remember, he's just doing a Polaroid tomorrow, then he'll tell you if you got the job. So be nice. . . ."

The next day when I got there, Terence Donovan looked at me and started laughing. "Oh. It's you again. Come here. What's your name?" From that moment on, he was very patient with me. Terence was a father, and he realized that I was just a frightened kid who needed help. He brought me tea, and showed me all his work, photos he'd taken of the most beautiful women in the world. "Okay. I'm going to show you some pictures. Come with me." He led me into another room full of shelves and drawers, and lying on a table was a calendar. He flipped through the pages, and on each page was the photograph of a different, stunningly gorgeous woman. "You see this? This is last year's Pirelli calendar. I do it every year. Except this year it's going to be different—just African women. Some pictures you'll be wearing clothes, but some might be no clothes." He went over everything with me, explaining how the whole process worked. By that point I felt comfortable that he wasn't just some dodgy, dirty old man. He said, "Okay, we're going to take the Polaroid now. Are you ready?"

As soon as Veronica told me how much I'd make I was ready, but now I was relaxed as well. "Yes, I'm ready." And from that moment on I was a complete professional. Stood on the mark—*whoosh*—off went the top, and I stared into the camera with confidence. Perfect! When he showed me the Polaroid, it reminded me of being back home in Africa. The shot was black and white, and very simple and honest—nothing tarty and corny; there was nothing pornographic about it. Instead, it was Waris as she'd grown up in the desert, looking just like a little girl child, tiny breasts exposed in the heat.

When I came home that night, I received the message from the agency saying I got the job and would be going to Bath next week. Veronica had left her home number. I called to explain that I was scheduled to work at McDonald's and couldn't afford not to, since I had no idea how long it would be before I'd see the money from my modeling job. But she saved me by saying if I needed money, she could give me an advance.

Since that day, I've never set foot in a McDonald's again. After I talked to Veronica, I hung up the phone and ran all over the Y. I told not only my friends about my new enterprise, but any stranger who would listen. Halwu said, "Oh, come on! Stop showing off, for God's sake! You're showing your tits, right?"

"Yeah, for fifteen hundred pounds!"

"For those little things? You should be ashamed," she laughed.

"But this is not like that. This is really nice! Not that nasty stuff . . . and we're going to Bath and stay in a big hotel."

"Well, I don't want to hear it—just stop telling everybody in the building about it, all right?"

The night before we left, I couldn't sleep at all, wishing it were morning; my packed duffel sat by the door. I still couldn't believe it—I'd never been anywhere, and these people were paying me money to go! Terence Donovan was sending a limousine to pick me up and bring me to Victoria Station. There the group—the photographers, assistants, art director, four other models, the makeup artist, hairstylist, and me—would assemble to take the train to Bath. I was the first person to arrive, because I was so nervous about missing the train. The next person who got there was Naomi Campbell.

When we arrived in Bath, we checked into the Royalton, which was like a palace; I was stunned to find out I'd have a huge room all to myself. But that first night, Naomi came to my room and asked if she could sleep with me. She was very young, and sweet, about sixteen or seventeen, and frightened to stay by herself. I said sure, because I enjoyed having the company. "Don't tell them, okay? They're going to be mad if they find out they're wasting all that money on my room and nobody's sleeping in it."

"Don't worry about it—just stay in my room." After years of experience, it came naturally to me to play the mother. In fact, my friends called me Mama, because I always wanted to mother everybody. "I'm not going to say anything, Naomi."

When we started to work in the morning, two girls would go first and get their hair and makeup done. Then, while they were on the set getting their pictures taken, the next two would get ready, and so on. The first morning that the hairstylist started working on me, I told him to chop it all off. Back then, I was pretty chunky for a model; I had all that nice juicy McDonald's meat on me. So I wanted my hair short, to make me look more fashionable. The stylist kept cutting and cutting, until almost nothing was left—my hair was about one inch long all over my head. Everyone said, "Ooohh, you look so different." But I decided I really wanted to shock people, and I said to the hairstylist, "You know what I'm going to do? I'm going to bleach my hair blond."

"Oh, God! Well, I'm not going to do it. You'd look wicked—mad!"

Naomi Campbell laughed and said, "Waris, you know what? One day you're going to be famous. And don't forget me then, okay?" Of course, the reverse came true, and she's the famous one.

We went on working like this for six days, and I couldn't believe I was getting paid for it. As soon as I got off in the evening, and the group would ask me what I wanted to do, my answer was always the same: go shopping. They would let me take the car, and the limo driver would drop me wherever I wanted, then come back and pick me up. When the job was done, my picture wound up being selected for the cover, which was a surprising honor and got me even more publicity.

We took the train back to London; as soon as we arrived, I jumped in the limo, and the driver asked where to drop me. I told him to take me to the agency. When I walked in the door, they said, "Guess what? There's another casting for you, and it's right around the corner. But hurry up—you have to go right now."

I protested about this, because I was tired. "I'll go tomorrow," I said.

"No, no. Tomorrow will be too late; it's over then. They're

looking for Bond girls for the new James Bond movie, *The Living Daylights*, with Timothy Dalton. Leave your bag here and let's go. We'll walk you over and show you where it is."

One of the guys from the agency took me around the corner and pointed to the building: "You see that door there, where all the people are going? That's the place." I went in, and it was a repeat of the day I went to Terence Donovan's studio, except worse. Inside was an army of girls, standing, leaning, sitting, gossiping, strutting, and striking poses.

The assistant said, "We're asking everybody to say a couple of words." This news sounded ominous to me, but I kept telling myself I was a professional model now, right? I'd worked for Terence Donovan on the Pirelli calendar. This was nothing I couldn't handle. When my turn came they ushered me into the studio and told me to stand on the mark.

I said, "I just want to tell you guys that I don't speak very good English."

They held up a cue card and said, "That's okay, you just have to read this." *Oh, my God—now what? I have to tell them I can't read? No, it's too much, it's too humiliating. I can't do it.*

Instead I said, "Excuse me. I have to go—I'll be right back." And I just walked out of the building and went to the agency for my bag. God knows how long the casting people waited for me before someone realized I wasn't coming back. At the agency I told them I hadn't gotten in yet; I just wanted to pick up my bag first, because it looked like it was going to be a long wait. This was around one or two in the afternoon, but I went home, dropped off my bag, then went out searching for a hairdresser. I wandered into a shop close to the Y, and a gentleman asked what he could do for me.

"Bleach my hair," I said.

The stylist raised his eyebrows. "Well, you know we can do it, but it's going to take a long time. And we close at eight."

"Okay. Then we have till eight."

"Yeah, but we have other appointments ahead of you." I

begged him till he finally gave in. He applied the peroxide and I immediately regretted my begging. My hair was so short that the chemicals started burning my head, and I felt like big hunks of my scalp were peeling away. But gritting my teeth, I waited it out. When the hairdresser washed my hair, it turned orange. So he had to do it again because the peroxide needed to stay on longer to remove the color. The second time it came out yellow. The third time I finally became a blonde.

I loved it, but as I walked back to the subway, little kids grabbed their mother's hands and cried, "Mommy, Mommy, Mommy, what is that thing? Is that a man or a woman?" I thought, *I'll be damned. Maybe I made a mistake here? I'm scaring the children.* But by the time I reached the Y, I decided I didn't give a shit, because my hair wasn't meant to impress the children. Being blond was something I wanted to try for *me* and I thought it looked bloody fabulous.

When I got home, I had message after message waiting for me from the agency. *Where are you? Everyone at the casting is still waiting for you. Are you coming back? They still want to see you. They're still waiting* . . . But the agency was closed, so I called Veronica at home. "Waris, where on earth did you go? They thought you went to the bathroom! Promise me you'll go back tomorrow?" She made me agree I'd go back the next morning.

Of course, what I had neglected to tell Veronica, the casting people noticed immediately: that yesterday I was an ordinary black woman, today I was a Somali with blond hair. The whole production stopped to stare at me. "Wow! That is amazing— you just did that last night?"

"Yeah."

"Oh, my. Love it. Love it—don't change it again, all right?"

I said, "Believe me, I'm not going through that torture again any time soon. By now my scalp is blond."

We picked up with the test where we'd left off the day before. "Are you worried about your English—is that the problem?"

"Yeah." I still couldn't bring myself to admit that I couldn't read.

"Okay. Well, just stand there, look right, look left. Say your name, where you're from, what agency you're with, and that's all." That much I could handle.

Afterward, since I was right around the corner from Crawford's, I decided it would be fun to drop by the agency and show them my hair. They went berserk. "What the fuck have you done to your hair!?"

"It's nice, isn't it?"

"Oh, my God, no, it's not nice! We can't book you now! You've got to consult with us before you do something like this to your appearance, Waris. The client has to know what they're getting—this isn't just *your* hair anymore that you can do anything you want with."

The casting people did, however, like my hair, and I got the Bond Girl job. But from that day forward the folks at the agency had a nickname for me: Guinness. Because I was dark with a white head on the top.

I was very excited about my new movie career, until one day I went by the agency and Veronica said, "Well, great news, Waris. *The Living Daylights* will be filmed in Morocco."

I froze.

"You know, unfortunately, I have something to tell you, which I really would rather not have to tell you. Remember the day you hired me and asked me if I had a passport? Well, I do, but I don't have a current visa, so if I leave England, I can't get back in."

"Waris, you lied to me! You have to have a valid passport to be a model or we can't use you; you have to travel all the time. God—you're not going to be able to do the job. We'll have to cancel."

"No, no. Don't do that—I'll think of something. I'll figure it out." Veronica gave me a disbelieving look, but said it was up to me. For the next few days I sat in my room thinking and thinking but nothing came to mind. I consulted all my friends, but the only solution anyone could think of was that I might marry someone, and I certainly had nobody to marry. I felt terrible, not only that my career was being flushed down the toilet, but that I'd lied to Veronica and let the agency down.

One night in the midst of this dilemma, I went downstairs to the pool at the Y. My friend Marilyn, a black woman who was born in London, worked there as a lifeguard. When I first moved in, I would come to the pool and just sit there and stare at it because I love the water. Finally, one night Marilyn asked me why I never went in, and I told her I couldn't swim. "Well, I can teach you," she said.

"Okay." I went to the deep end of the pool, took a deep breath, and dived in. I figured since she was a lifeguard, she could save me. But guess what? Underneath the water, I swam like a fish all the way to the other end of the pool.

I came up with the biggest grin on my face. "I did it! I can't believe, I did it!"

But she was angry. "Why did you tell me you couldn't swim?"

"I never swam in my life!" After that episode, we became good friends. She lived with her mother on the other side of the city, and sometimes, when she got off work late at night, she'd be too tired to make the long journey home. So she would stay in my room.

Marilyn was a generous, lovely person, and as I swam in the pool that evening, trying to forget my passport troubles, the solution came to me. I came to the surface and pushed up my goggles. "Marilyn," I panted, "I need your passport."

"What? What are you talking about?" I explained my problem. "You're out of your fucking mind, Waris! Do you know what's going to happen? They're going to catch you, deport you for life, and put me in jail. Now, what am I risking all that for? So you can be in some stupid James Bond movie? I don't think so."

"Oh, come on, Marilyn. It's fun, an adventure—take the risk. We'll go to the post office and I'll apply for a passport in your name; I'll forge your signature, and put my picture on it. I don't have much time, but I can get a temporary passport in just a couple of days. *Please, Marilyn!* It's my big chance to be in the movies!"

Finally, after hours of pleading and begging, the day before I was scheduled to fly to Morocco, she gave in. I had my photo taken, then we went to the post office; an hour later I had my British passport. But all the way home, she was worried sick. I kept saying, "Cheer up, Marilyn. Come on, it'll be okay. You've just got to have faith."

"Faith my ass. I have faith that this one stupid incident can ruin my whole life." That night we went to her mother's house to spend the night. I suggested that we rent some videos and get some Chinese takeout and relax. But when we got to Marilyn's, she said, "Waris. I can't do it. It's too dangerous. Give me back the passport." I sorrowfully handed it to her, watching my movie career disappear into the realm of lost fantasies. "You stay here— I'm going to hide it," she said. She took it upstairs to her room.

I said, "Okay, girl. If it makes you feel like this, there's no point in suffering. If you think something will go wrong, then we shouldn't do it." But that night, as soon as she went to sleep, I started scouring her room. She had hundreds of books in there, and I knew that's where it had to be hidden. One by one, I opened them and shook them. The car was coming to her house in the morning to pick me up and take me to the airport, so I was moving fast. And suddenly the passport fell out at my feet. Grabbing it up quietly, I stuck it in my duffel, then went to bed. In the morning I woke up and sneaked downstairs before the driver came to ring the bell, so he wouldn't wake anybody up. It was cold outside, but I stood on the sidewalk shivering until the car came at seven, then headed to Heathrow.

Getting out of England was no problem. In Morocco, my movie career consisted of a couple of scenes where I was supposed to be what the script called "a beautiful girl lying around the pool." Then I was in another scene where we were sitting inside this fantastic house in Casablanca having tea, yet for some reason all the women were naked. James Bond flew through the bloody roof, and we threw our hands up to our faces and screamed, "Ahhh, oh, my God!" But I thought, *Well, I'm not complaining. Since I didn't get a speaking part, at least that means I don't have to worry about the fact that I can't read.*

The rest of the time we just lounged around the house, sat by the pool, ate and ate, and did nothing at all. I stayed in the sun the whole time, so thrilled to see it again after living in foggy London. Not knowing how to mingle with the movie people, I stayed mostly by myself; they were all very handsome and intimidating, spoke perfect English, and seemed to know each other—gossiping about this job and that job. I was just thrilled to be back in Africa again; in the evening, I'd go sit outside with the mamas cooking colorful food for their families. I couldn't speak the language, but we'd smile, and I'd say one word of Arabic, they'd say one word of English, and we'd laugh.

One day the film crew came around and said, "Anybody want to go to the camel races? Come on, we're getting a group together." After standing around watching the races for a while, I asked one of the Arab jockeys if I could ride, too. In a mangled combination of Arabic and English we communicated; he informed me that, oh no, women weren't allowed to ride the camels.

"I bet I can beat you," I said. "Come on, I'll show you— you're afraid for me to ride because I'm going to win!" This infuriated him—that this little girl would challenge him—and that's when he decided to let me race. The word spread through the movie crew that Waris was going to enter the next race; everybody gathered around and a few people tried to talk me out of it. I informed them to get their money out and bet on Waris, because I was going to teach these Moroccan guys a lesson. There were about ten Arab men seated on their camels at the starting line, and me. When the race began, we took off and flew. It was a terrifying ride, because I was not familiar with this camel and didn't really know how to make him "kick." Camels not only hurtle forward at a fast clip, but bounce up and down and side to side, so I was hanging on for my life. I knew if I fell, I would be trampled to death.

When the race was finished, I had come in second place. The James Bond people were astonished, and I could tell I'd gained a new, if weird respect, especially as they collected their winning bets. "How did you know how to do that?" one girl asked me.

"Easy. When you're born on top of a camel, you know how to ride one," I laughed.

However, the camel race demanded no courage compared to what was awaiting me when I returned to Heathrow. As we exited the plane, we lined up for customs; as the line inched forward, everyone got their passports out. The officials would yell out, "NEXT!" and each time it was the most excruciating torture to hear that word, because it meant I was one step closer to being arrested.

The British officials are always harsh enough letting you into England; but if you're African and black, they're doubly tough. You know they'll be scanning your passport with razor eyes. I felt so sick I wanted to faint—and began to fantasize about lying down on the floor and dying so I wouldn't have to go through this agony anymore. *God*, I prayed, *please help me. If I live through this, I promise I'll never do anything this stupid again.*

I was almost there, if my knees didn't give out. Then suddenly an obnoxious male model named Geoffrey grabbed my passport from my hand. He was a smart-aleck bastard anyway, who delighted in making other people miserable, and this time he couldn't have found a more vulnerable target. "Oh, please, please—" I tried to grab it back from him, but he was much taller than I was and held it up where I couldn't reach it.

Everyone throughout the trip had called me Waris; they all knew my name was Waris Dirie. Geoffrey opened the passport and shrieked, "Oh, my God. Listen to this—listen to this, everybody. Guess what her name is? MARILYN MONROE."

"Please give that to me—" I was shaking by now.

He ran around in circles, doubled over laughing, then began showing the whole gang my passport. "Her name is Marilyn Monroe! Check this shit out! What the fuck? What's the story here, girl? No wonder you bleached your hair!"

I had no idea there was another Marilyn Monroe. To me, she was simply my friend, the lifeguard at the Y. Luckily, I didn't even know about the added concern that I was walking around with a passport bearing my photo and the name of a famous movie star. At that moment, my biggest worry was that my passport said I was Marilyn Monroe, born in London, yet I barely spoke a word of English. *I'm dead . . . It's over . . . I'm dead . . . It's over . . .* were the words ringing through my brain as my whole body poured a river of sweat.

All the James Bond people joined in the game: "Hey, so what's your real name? Now, really—where are you from? Did you know that people born in the middle of London don't speak English?" They were just ribbing the piss out of me. This Geoffrey jerk finally handed back my passport. I went back to the end of the line, letting all of them go through ahead of me, hoping they'd be gone by the time it was my turn.

"NEXT!"

As the rest of the film crew went through customs, no one went on about their business, running off to hop in the car as they normally would have after a long trip. No. They waited, huddled around in a group just beyond the customs booth, to see how I was going to get out of this one.

Pull yourself together, Waris, girl. You can do it. I walked up and handed the customs clerk my passport with a dazzling smile. "Hello!" I called out, then held my breath. I knew better than to say one more word, because then he'd find out my English was a joke.

"Nice day, isn't it?"

"Umm." I nodded and smiled. He handed me my passport and I sailed by. The James Bond crew stood there looking at me in astonishment. I wanted to collapse, exhale, and fall down on the floor, but I flew past them too, knowing I wasn't safe until I got out of the airport. *Just keep moving, Waris. Get out of Heathrow alive.*

12.

THE DOCTORS

While I was still living at the YMCA, I spent an afternoon in the pool downstairs, swimming laps. After I finished, I dressed in the locker room, and was heading back upstairs when I heard someone calling my name from the Y's little café. It was a guy I knew who also lived in the building. His name was William and he motioned for me to come in. "Waris, have a seat. Would you like something to eat?"

William was eating a cheese sandwich, and I said, "Yeah, I'll have one of those, please." My English was still pretty weak, but I could make out the gist of what he was saying. While we ate, he asked me if I'd like to go to the movies. This was not the first time he'd asked me out. William was young, handsome, white, and always very sweet. But as he talked, I stopped hearing what he was saying. Instead I sat staring at him, watching his lips move, and my mind began running like a computer:

Go to the movies with him

If only he knew about me
Oh, imagine what it would be like to have a boyfriend
It might be nice
Someone to talk to
Someone to love me
But if I go to the movies
He'll want to kiss me
Then he'll want to have sex
And if I agree
He'll find out I'm not like other girls
I'm damaged
Or if I disagree
He'll be angry and we'll have a fight
Don't go
It's not worth the heartache
Say no
If only he knew about me, he'd realize it has nothing to do with him.

I smiled and shook my head. "No, thanks. I have too much work." The hurt look that I knew would come, came, and I shrugged, saying to both of us: *There's nothing I can do.*

This problem began when I moved to the Y. When I lived with my family, I was normally never around strange men unchaperoned. A man who came to my parents, or Auntie Sahru's, or Uncle Mohammed's, would either know our culture and not attempt to ask me on a date, or would be dealt with by the family. But since I left my uncle's house, I had been alone. And for the first time I was forced to cope with these situations by myself. The Y was a building chock-full of young, single men. Going to clubs with Halwu I met more men. Modeling I met more men still.

But I was interested in none of them. The thought of having sex with a man never crossed my mind, but unfortunately, after some of my awful experiences, I knew it crossed theirs. Although I've always wondered, I can't imagine what my life would be like if I hadn't been circumcised. I like men and I'm a very emotional, loving person. At that time, it had been six years since I ran away from my father, and the loneliness had been hard for me; I missed my family. And someday I hoped to have a husband and family of my own. But as long as I was sewn up, I was very much closed to the idea of a relationship, shut away into myself. It was as if the stitches prevented any man from entering me—physically or emotionally.

The other problem that prevented me from having a relationship with a man came up when I realized I was different from other women, particularly Englishwomen. After I arrived in London, it gradually dawned on me that not all girls had had done to them what had been done to me. When I lived with my cousins at Uncle Mohammed's house, sometimes I would be in the bathroom with the other girls. I was amazed when they peed quickly in a heavy stream, whereas it took me about ten minutes to urinate. The tiny hole the circumciser had left me only permitted the urine to escape one drop at a time. "Waris, why do you pee like that—what's wrong with you?" I didn't want to tell them because I assumed when they got back to Somalia they would be circumcised, too, so I just laughed it off.

However, my periods were no laughing matter. From the very beginning, when I was around eleven or twelve years old, they were a nightmare. They began one day when I was alone out tending my sheep and goats. The day was unbearably hot, and I sat weakly under a tree, feeling even more uncomfortable because my stomach hurt. I wondered, *What is this pain? Maybe I'm pregnant? Maybe I'm going to have a baby? But I haven't been with a man, so how can I be pregnant?* The pressure grew and grew, and so did my fear. About an hour later I went to pee and saw blood. I thought I was dying.

Leaving the animals grazing in the bush, I flew home, and

ran to my mother crying and screaming, "I'm dying! Oh, Mama, I'm dying!"

"What are you talking about?"

"I'm bleeding, Mama—I'm going to die!"

She stared at me hard. "No, you're not going to die. It's all right. It's your period." I had never heard of periods—knew nothing about any of it.

"Can you please explain this to me—tell me what you're talking about?" My mother explained the process as I writhed around in misery, holding my abdomen. "But how do I stop this pain? Because, you know, it *feels* like I'm dying!"

"Waris, you can't stop it. You just have to let it go. Wait until it's ready to leave."

However, I wasn't prepared to accept that solution. Looking for something that would bring me relief, I went back into the desert and started digging a hole under a tree. The motion felt good and gave me something to take my mind off my pain. I dug and dug with a stick until I had a spot deep enough to bury the bottom half of my body. Then I climbed in, packing the dirt in around me; the underground hole was cooler, sort of like an ice pack, and I would rest there during the heat of the day.

Digging a hole in the ground became the method I would use for coping with my period each month. Oddly enough, later I found out that my sister Aman had done the same thing. But this treatment had its drawbacks. One day my father came walking by and saw his daughter half buried under a tree. Viewed from a distance, I looked like I'd been cut off at the waist and had been sat on the sand. "What the hell are you doing?" On hearing his voice, I automatically tried to jump out of the hole, but since the dirt was packed tightly around me, I didn't get very far. Struggling out, I clawed with my hands to get my legs free. Papa started laughing hysterically. I was too shy to explain why I did it, and afterward he kept making jokes about it. "If you want to bury yourself alive, do it properly. I mean, come on, what was that halfway business?" Later, he asked my mother about my strange behavior. He worried his daughter was turning into some kind of burrowing animal—a mole obsessed with tunneling underground—but Mama explained the situation.

However, as my mother had predicted, there was nothing I could do to stop the pain. Although I didn't understand it at the time, the menstrual blood backed up in my body the same way the urine did. But since it was continuously flowing—or trying to—for several days, the pressure of the blockage was excruciating. The blood came out one drop at a time; as a result, my periods usually lasted for at least ten days.

This problem reached a crisis while I was living with my uncle Mohammed. Early one morning, I prepared his breakfast as usual. Then carrying the tray from the kitchen to the dining room table where he waited, I suddenly blacked out, and the dishes crashed to the floor around me. Uncle ran to me and started slapping my face, trying to bring me around. I began to regain consciousness and, as if he were far away, I heard him crying, "Maruim! Maruim! She's fainted!"

When I came to, Aunt Maruim asked me what was wrong, and I told her I'd gotten my period that morning. "Well, this is not right, we have to take you to the doctor. I'll make an appointment with my doctor this afternoon."

I told Auntie's doctor that my periods were very bad, and whenever I got them, I started passing out. The pain paralyzed me, and I didn't know what to do about it. "Can you help me? Please—is there something you can do? Because I can't stand it anymore." However, I didn't mention to him that I'd been circumcised. I didn't even know how to begin a discussion of that topic. Back then I was still a girl, and all the issues associated with my physical condition were mixed with ignorance, confusion, and shame. And I wasn't sure my circumcision was the source of the problem, since I still thought what happened to me happened to all girls. My mother hadn't thought my pain unusual, because all the women she had ever known had been circumcised, and they all went through this agony. It's considered part of the burden of being a woman.

Since the doctor didn't examine me, he didn't find out my secret. "The only thing I can give you for pain is birth control pills. That will stop the pain because it will stop your periods."

Hallelujah! I began taking the pills, even though I didn't really like the idea. I'd heard from my cousin Basma that they were bad for you. But within the month, the pain stopped and so did much of my bleeding. Because the drug tricked my body into thinking it was pregnant, other unexpected things happened also. My breasts grew; my ass grew; my face filled out, and my weight exploded. These drastic changes in my body seemed extremely weird and unnatural. Deciding I'd rather deal with the pain, I stopped taking the pills. And deal with the pain I did, because it all came right back again, fiercer than ever.

Later, I visited a second doctor to see if he could help. But that experience was a repeat of the first; he wanted to give me birth control pills as well. I explained that I had tried that option, but I didn't like the side effects. However, without the pills I couldn't function for several days each month; I simply went to bed and wanted to die so the suffering would stop. Did he know of another solution? The doctor said, "Well, what do you expect? When women take birth control pills, for the most part their periods stop. When women have periods, they have pain. Take your pick." When the third doctor repeated this same advice, I realized I needed to do something besides visit new doctors.

I said to Auntie, "Maybe I need to see a special kind of doctor?"

She looked at me sharply. "No," she said emphatically. "And by the way—what are you telling these men?"

"Nothing. That I just want to stop the pain, that's all." I knew the unspoken message of her comment: circumcision is our African custom—and not something you discuss with these white men.

I began to understand, however, that this was exactly what I was going to have to do. Or suffer and live like an invalid for one third of each month. I also understood that this action would never be accepted by my family. My next step became clear: I would have to secretly go back to the doctor, and tell him I'd been circumcised. Perhaps then one of them could help me.

I chose the first doctor, Dr. Macrae, because he was located in a big hospital and, I reasoned, would have the facilities if I needed surgery. When I called for an appointment, I had to wait a whole agonizing month before I could get in. When the day came, I made some excuse to Auntie for my absence, and went to Dr. Macrae's office. I said to him, "There's something I haven't told you. I'm from Somalia and I—I—" It was terrible for me to try to explain this horrible secret in my broken English. "I been circumcised."

He didn't even let me finish the sentence. "Go get changed. I want to examine you." He saw the look of terror on my face. "It's okay." He called in his nurse, and she showed me where to change, how to put the gown on.

When we went back into the examining room, I really questioned what I'd gotten myself into this time. The thought that a girl from my country would sit in this strange place, spread her legs, and let a white man look in there . . . well, it was the most shameful thing I could imagine. The doctor kept trying to get my knees apart. "Relax. It's all right—I'm a doctor. The nurse is right here—she's standing right there." I craned my neck around to look in the direction his finger was pointing. She smiled reassuringly at me and I finally gave in. I forced myself to think about something else, pretend I wasn't here, but was back walking in the desert with my goats on a beautiful day.

When he finished, he asked the nurse if there was someone in the hospital who could speak Somali; she said yes, there was a Somali woman working downstairs. But when she came back, she brought a Somali man instead, because she couldn't find the woman. I thought, *Oh, beautiful! Here's the rotten luck, to discuss this horrible business using a Somali man to translate! How much worse could it get?*

Dr. Macrae said, "Explain to her that she's closed up way too much—I don't even know how she's made it this far. We need to operate on her as soon as possible." Right away, I could see the Somali man wasn't happy. He pursed his lips and glared at the doctor. Between the fact that I did understand some English, and the Somali man's attitude, I sensed that something was not right.

He said to me, "Well, if you really want it, they can open you up." I just stared at him. "But do you know this is against your culture? Does your family know you're doing this?"

"No. To tell you the truth, no."

"Who do you live with?"

"My aunt and uncle."

"Do they know you're doing this?"

"No."

"Well, the first thing I'd do is discuss it with them." I nodded, thinking: *That's the response of a typical African man. Thanks for your good advice, brother. That will put an end to the whole business.*

Dr. Macrae added that he couldn't do the operation right away; I'd need to make an appointment. I realized then that I couldn't do it, because Auntie would find out. "Yeah. I'll do that—I'll call for an appointment." Of course, over a year went by and I never called.

Immediately after my family returned to Somalia, I called and made an appointment, but the soonest I could get was two months. As the two months ticked by, I remembered the horror of my circumcision. I thought the surgery would be a repeat of that process, and the more I thought about it, I decided I couldn't go through that again. When the day came, I simply never went to the hospital and never called.

By this point I was living at the Y. The problems with my periods hadn't decreased, but now I was having to earn my living outside the home. You couldn't just miss a week of work each month and hope to keep a job. I struggled along, but my friends at the Y saw I was in bad shape. Marilyn kept asking me what was wrong. I explained to her that I'd been circumcised as a girl in Somalia.

But Marilyn was raised in London, and she couldn't fathom what I was talking about. "Why don't you show me, Waris? I really don't know what you're talking about. Did they cut you here? This? That? What did they do?"

Finally one day I pulled my pants down and showed her. I'll never forget the look on her face. Tears poured down her cheeks as she turned away. I felt so desperate, because I thought: *Oh, my God, is it really that bad?* The first words out of her mouth were "Waris, do you feel *anything*?"

"What are you talking about?"

She just shook her head. "You know, do you remember how you looked when you were a little girl? Before they did this?"

"Yes."

"Well, that's how I am now. You're not the same." Now I knew for sure. No longer did I need to wonder—or maybe even hope—that all women had been mutilated the way I had. Now I knew for certain that I was different. I didn't wish my suffering on anyone else, but I didn't want to be on my own. "So this hasn't happened to you, to you and your mother?"

She shook her head and began crying again. "It's horrible, Waris. I can't believe that anybody would do this to you."

"Oh, come on, please don't make me feel sad."

"*I* feel sad. Sad and angry. I'm crying in a way because I can't believe there are people in the world who would do this to a little girl."

We sat there in silence for a few moments, and while Marilyn continued to sob quietly I couldn't look at her. Then I decided I'd had enough. "Well, fuck it. I'm going to have this surgery. I'm going to call this doctor tomorrow. At least I can enjoy going to the bathroom. That's all I can enjoy, but at least that much."

"I'll go with you, Waris. I'll be right there. I promise."

Marilyn called the doctor's office and made the appointment for me; this time I had to wait a month. During that time, I kept saying, "Girl, you sure you're coming with me?"

"Don't worry. I'm coming. I'll be right there." When the morning came for surgery, she got me up early and we went to the hospital. The nurse led me into the room. Ah, there it was: the table. When I saw the operating table, I nearly turned around and ran out of the building. It was better than a rock in the bush, but I had little hope the procedure would feel much better. However, Dr. Macrae gave me an anesthetic for pain— something I wished I'd had when the Killer Woman butchered me. Marilyn held my hand while I went to sleep.

When I woke up, they had moved me into a double room with a woman who had just given birth. This lady, along with all the people I'd meet at lunchtime in the cafeteria, kept asking me, "So, what are you here for?"

What could I say? Confess, "Oh, I came to have surgery on my vagina. My pussy was just way too tight!" I never told anyone the truth. I said I had a stomach bug. And even though my recovery process was greatly improved over that of my circumcision, some of my worst memories of that time were repeated. Every time I had to pee, the same old thing: salt and hot water. But at least the nurses let me have a bath and I'd soak in the hot water. Ahhhh. They gave me painkillers, so it wasn't so bad, but I was really glad when it was over.

Dr. Macrae did a fine job, and I've always been grateful to him. He told me, "You know, you're not alone. Let me tell you,

I have women come in here with this same problem all the time. A lot of women from the Sudan, Egypt, Somalia. Some of them are pregnant and they're terrified because trying to give birth while they're sewn up is dangerous. There can be a lot of complications—the baby can suffocate trying to exit the tight opening, or the mother can bleed to death. So, without the permission of their husbands or their family they come to me, and I do my bit. I do my best."

Within two or three weeks I was back to normal. Well, not exactly normal, but more like a woman who hadn't been circumcised. Waris was a new woman. I could sit down on the toilet and pee—*whoosh!* There's no way to explain what a new freedom that was.

13.

PASSPORT
DILEMMA

When I returned from my movie debut as a Bond Girl, I told the driver to take me straight to Marilyn Monroe's house. Like a coward, I hadn't called my friend after I'd left for Morocco, but instead had decided to let her cool off until I returned. Standing on her stoop with a sack full of presents, I nervously rang the bell. She opened the front door, grinned from ear to ear, then rushed forward to hug me. "You did it! You crazy bitch, you did it!" Marilyn forgave me for stealing the fraudulent passport; she said she was so impressed that I had the guts to pull the whole caper off that she couldn't stay mad. But I agreed never to put either one of us through the danger of using her passport again, especially after my torture passing through customs at Heathrow.

I was glad that Marilyn forgave me, because she was indeed a good friend. And once again, I had to call on that friendship. When I returned home to London, I thought my modeling career was just beginning—especially after the back-to-back successes of working with Terence Donovan and being in a

James Bond movie. But as if by magic, my modeling career vanished over night, disappearing as suddenly and mysteriously as it had begun. No more working at McDonald's for me, but also no more living at the YMCA. With no work, I couldn't afford to keep my room there, and was forced to move into the house with Marilyn and her mother. This arrangement pleased me much more in many ways—living in a real home, and being part of their family. I wound up staying with them for seven months, and even though they didn't complain, I knew I'd outstayed my welcome. I got a few little modeling jobs here and there, but still was not making enough money to support myself. I moved in with another friend, a Chinese man named Frankie, who was a friend of my hairdresser. Frankie owned a big house—well, to me it was big because it had two bedrooms. He generously offered to let me stay there while I tried to get my career going.

In 1987, shortly after I moved in with Frankie, *The Living Daylights* came out. A couple of weeks later, another friend took me out on Christmas Eve; everyone in London was celebrating, and caught up in the mood, I came home very late. As soon as my head touched the pillow, I was asleep. But a steady tapping on my bedroom window woke me. Looking outside I saw the friend who'd just dropped me off, holding a newspaper. He was trying to say something, but I couldn't understand him, so I opened the window.

"Waris! You're on the cover of *The Sunday Times*!"

"Oh . . . " I rubbed my eyes. "Honestly—I am?"

"Yeah! Take a look." He held up the paper and there was a three-quarter shot of my face filling the whole cover. It was larger than life-size, with my blond hair ablaze and a determined look on my face.

"That's nice . . . I'm going back to bed now . . . sleep," and I stumbled to my bed. By noon, however, I'd realized the possibilities of that publicity. Surely being on the cover of *The Sunday Times* of London would generate some action. In the meantime, I hustled. I ran all over London going to castings, pestered my booker, and finally switched modeling agencies, but nothing improved.

My new agency said, "Well, Waris, there's simply not much of a market for a black model in London. You have to travel for jobs—Paris, Milan, New York." I was all for traveling, except for the same old problem: my passport dilemma. The agency said they'd heard of an attorney, Harold Wheeler, who had been able to help several immigrants with their passports. Why didn't I talk to him?

I went to this Harold Wheeler's office and discovered that he wanted an extortionate amount of money to help me—two thousand pounds. Still, I reasoned, since I would be able to travel and work, I could make that money back in no time. As it stood now, I was quickly going nowhere. I scraped together the money from every possible source, eventually raising the two-thousand-pound fee. But I was concerned about giving him all my borrowed cash, then finding out he was a crook.

Making sure to leave my cash at home, I made my second appointment, and took Marilyn with me for her opinion. I rang the intercom and Wheeler's secretary answered, then buzzed us into the building. My friend waited in the lobby while I met with Wheeler in his office.

I spoke bluntly: "Tell me the truth. I just want to know if this passport I'm getting is going to be worth two thousand pounds. Am I going to be able to travel all over the world legally? I don't want to wind up stranded in some godforsaken place and get deported. And where are you getting this thing from?"

"No, no, no, I'm afraid I can't talk about my sources. You must leave that to me. If you want a passport, my dear, I can certainly get you a passport. And you have my word, it will be perfectly legal. After we begin the process it will take two weeks. My secretary will give you a ring when it's ready." *Great! That means two weeks from now I can just bugger off anyplace I like, anytime.*

"Well, okay, that sounds good," I said. "What do we do next?" Wheeler explained how I would marry an Irish national, and he just happened to have such an individual in mind. The two thousand pounds would go to the Irishman in return for his services. Wheeler would keep only a small fee for himself. He wrote down the date and time of my appointment; I was to meet my new husband at the registry office, and bring one hundred and fifty pounds in cash for additional expenses.

"You'll be meeting a Mr. O'Sullivan," Wheeler advised in his proper British accent. He continued to write as he talked. "He is the gentleman you'll be marrying. Oh, and—by the way— congratulations." He glanced up and gave me a slight smile.

Later, I asked Marilyn if she thought I should trust this guy. She said, "Well, he has a nice office in a nice building in a nice neighborhood. He has his name on the door. He has a professional secretary. He looks legitimate enough to me."

My trusted friend Marilyn also came with me as a witness on my wedding day. Waiting outside the registry office, we watched an old man with a withered red face, unruly white hair, and ragged clothes zigzag down the sidewalk. We were laughing until he started up the registry steps. Marilyn and I looked at each other in shock, then back at him. "Are you Mr. O'Sullivan?" I ventured.

"In the flesh. That's me name." He lowered his voice. "Are you the one?" I nodded. "You got the money, lass—did you bring the money?"

"Yes."

"One hundred fifty quid?"

"Yes."

"Good girl. Well, then, hurry up, hurry up. Let's go. Time's a-wastin'." My new husband-to-be reeked of whiskey, and was obviously completely and thoroughly soused.

As we followed him inside, I muttered to Marilyn, "Is he going to live long enough for me to get my passport?"

The registrar began performing the ceremony, but I was having a hard time concentrating. I was constantly being distracted by Mr. O'Sullivan weaving unsteadily on his feet; and sure enough, as the registrar said, "Do you, Waris, take this man—" he collapsed to the floor with a heavy thud. At first I thought he'd died till I realized he was breathing heavily through his open mouth. I knelt down and started shaking him, yelling, "Mr. O'Sullivan, wake up!" But he refused.

I rolled my eyes at Marilyn and cried, "Oh, great, my wedding day!" and she fell against the wall laughing, holding her stomach. "Just my luck! My dear husband-to-be passes out on me at the altar." Presented with such a ridiculous situation, I figured we might as well have some fun, and I twisted it for all I could get.

The registrar put both hands on her knees and bent down to examine my fiancé, peering over the top of her tiny half glasses. "Is he going to be all right?"

I wanted to shout at her, "How the fuck should I know?" but realized that would be giving away the game. "Wake up, come on, WAKE UP!" I had resorted to slapping his face fairly soundly by now. "Please—somebody get me some water. Somebody do *something*!" I pleaded with a laugh. The registrar brought a cup of water and I threw it in the old man's face.

"Ugh . . ." He began snorting and grunting and finally his eyes flickered open. With some serious tugging and pushing we were able to get him to his feet.

"My God, let's get on with it," I mumbled, worried that he'd keel over again. I held on to my beloved's arm with an iron grip until we finished the ceremony. Back on the sidewalk, Mr. O'Sullivan asked for the one hundred fifty pounds, and I got his address, just in case I had any problems. He lunged off down the street singing a little ditty with the last of my money in his pocket.

One week later Harold Wheeler himself called to say my passport was ready; I gleefully rushed down to his office to pick it up. He handed me the document: an Irish passport with a photograph of my black face and the name Waris O'Sullivan. I was no expert on passports, but it looked a little weird. No, it looked *really* weird. Rinky-dink, as if somebody had made it in the basement. "This is it? I mean, this is a legal passport? I can travel with this?"

"Oh, yes." Wheeler nodded his head emphatically. "Irish, you see. It's an Irish passport."

"Ummm." I turned it over and examined the back cover, flipped through the pages. "Well. So long as it does the job, who cares how it looks?"

I didn't wait long to put it to the test. My agency set up bookings for me in Paris and Milan and I applied for my travel visas. But a couple of days later, I received a letter. When I glanced at the return address, I felt ill. The letter was from the immigration office, saying they wanted to see me right away. I considered all kinds of wild options, but in the end I knew there was nothing to be done, except go see them. I also knew they had the power to deport me immediately—or send me to jail. Good-bye, London. Good-bye, Paris. Good-bye, Milan. Good-bye, modeling. Hello, camels.

The day after I received the letter, I took the tube from Frankie's house to the immigration office, and wandering through the huge government building, I felt like I was walking into a tomb. When I found the right office, I was met by the most deadly serious faces I'd ever seen. "Sit here," ordered a stone-faced man. They put me in a completely isolated room and began asking me questions. "What is your name? What was your name before you married? Where are you from? How did you get this passport? What was his name? How much money did you pay?" I knew one little wrong answer and they would be putting handcuffs on old Waris. Meanwhile, the immigration officials were recording every word I said. So I trusted my instincts and didn't tell them much. When I needed to stall and think of an answer, I relied on my perfectly natural talent, pretending to be confused by the language barrier.

Immigration kept my passport and told me that in order to get it back I had to bring my husband in for an interview—not what I was hoping to hear. In the end, though, I was able to get out of their office without telling them about Harold Wheeler. I figured to get my money back from this thief before the government picked him up, or that would be the end of my two thousand pounds.

I left immigration, marched straight to his swanky office, and rang the intercom. When his secretary answered, I said it was Waris Dirie to see Mr. Wheeler and it was urgent. But surprisingly, Mr. Wheeler was not in, so she refused to open the door. Day after day I came to his office and called on the phone screaming, but his loyal secretary protected the rat. Playing private detective, I hid outside his building all day long, waiting to pounce on him when he walked by. But he had disappeared.

In the meantime, I had to produce Mr. O'Sullivan for the immigration board. His address was in Croydon, south London, an immigrant neighborhood where a lot of Somalis live. I took the train as far as I could, then had to take a cab the rest of the way, because trains don't go there. Walking down the street alone, I kept looking over my shoulder, really not happy to be there. I found the address, a broken-down tenement, and knocked on the door. No answer. I walked around the side of the house and strained to look in the window, but couldn't see anything. Where could he be—where would he go in the daytime? I wondered. Ah—the pub. I started walking, and when I came to the closest pub, I went inside and found Mr. O'Sullivan sitting at the bar. "Remember me?" I asked. The old man looked over his shoulder, then quickly resumed his position staring straight ahead at the bottles of liquor behind the bar. *Think fast, Waris.* I had to tell him the bad news, and beg him to come to immigration with me; I knew he wouldn't go for it. "Here's the story, Mr. O'Sullivan. Immigration took my passport away. They want to talk to you, just ask you a couple of quick questions before they'll give it back. Make sure we're really married, you know. I can't find this damn attorney—he's disappeared, so I've got nobody to help me." Still staring straight ahead, he took a swig of whiskey and shook his head. "Look, I gave you *two thousand pounds* to help me get my passport!"

This got his attention. He turned to stare at me, his mouth open in amazement. "You gave me one-fifty, love. I never had two thousand pounds in me life, or I wouldn't be hanging around the likes of Croydon."

"I gave Harold Wheeler two thousand pounds for you to marry me!"

"Well, he didn't give it to me. If you're foolish enough to give that man two thousand quid that's your problem—not mine." I kept begging, pleading with him to help me, but he wasn't interested. I promised I'd take him in a cab, he wouldn't even have to take the train to the immigration office. But he wouldn't budge from his bar stool.

Searching for the right approach to motivate him, I offered, "Look, I'll pay you. I'll give you more money. After we visit immigration, we'll go to the pub, and you can drink all you want." This offer received skeptical interest, as he turned to me and raised his eyebrows. *Push it home, Waris.* "Whiskey, lots and lots of whiskeys, shots lined up all the way down the bar. Okay? I'll come to your house tomorrow, and we'll take a taxi to London. It will only take a few minutes, a couple of quick questions— and then we'll head straight for the pub. Right?" He nodded his head and went back to staring at the bottles of spirits behind the counter.

The next morning, I returned to Croydon and knocked on

the old man's door. But there was no answer. I walked down the deserted street to the pub and went inside, but the only person there was the barkeep, wearing a white apron and drinking a cup of coffee while he read the paper. "Have you seen Mr. O'Sullivan today?"

He shook his head. "Too early for him, love." I walked quickly back to the lying bum's house and pounded on the door. Still no answer, so I sat down on the front steps, which reeked of piss, and I put my hand over my nose. While I sat there trying to decide what to do next, two tough-looking guys in their twenties walked up and stopped in front of me.

"Who're you?" one of them grunted at me. "And why are ya sittin' on me old man's stoop?"

"Oh, hi," I said pleasantly. "I don't know if you know, but I'm married to your father."

They both glared at me, and the bigger of the two shouted, "What! What the fuck are ya talking about?"

"Look, you know, I'm in a complete mess and I need your father's help. All I want is for him to come with me to this office in the city, and answer a couple of questions. They took my passport away, and I need to get it back, so please . . ."

"Piss off, you fucking cunt!"

"Hey, look! I gave that old man all my money," I said, pointing to his front door, "and I'm not leaving without him." However, his son had other ideas. He jerked a club out of his coat and pulled it back menacingly, like he was going to break my skull.

"Oh, yeah? Well, we're going to fuck you up. We'll teach you to come around here telling your lies—" His brother laughed and grinned, and I stared at his smile, missing a few teeth. That was enough for me. I knew these guys had nothing to lose. They could beat me to death right here on the doorstep, and nobody would know—or care. I jumped up and ran. They chased me for a couple of blocks; then, satisfied that they'd scared me away, they stopped.

But when I got home that day, I decided to go back to Croydon again, and keep going back until I found the old man. I had no other choice. By this point, Frankie was not only letting me live with him without paying rent, but he was buying my food, too. Added to that, I was borrowing money from my other friends for expenses, and that situation couldn't go on much longer. I'd thrown away all my money on that crook posing as an immigration attorney, and without a passport, I couldn't work. So what did I have to lose? A few teeth if I wasn't careful, but I decided I had to be smarter than those punks, and that didn't seem too difficult.

I went back the next afternoon and quietly circled the neighborhood, making sure not to stop in front of the old man's house. I found a little park and sat down on a bench, and in a few minutes Mr. O'Sullivan himself came strolling past. For some unknown reason, he was in a jolly mood and happy to see me. He quickly agreed to get in a taxi with me and head to London. "You're going to pay me, yeah?" I nodded. "And then you'll buy us a drink, lass?"

"I'll buy you all the drinks you need when we're finished. But first you have to be a little bit normal when you talk to these immigration people. They're complete bastards, you know. *Then afterwards* we'll go to the pub. . . ."

When we walked into immigration the agent took one look at Mr. O'Sullivan and, with a very grim face, said, "This is your husband?"

"Yes."

"Okay, Mrs. O'Sullivan, let's stop playing these games. What's the story?" I sighed, realizing that there was no point going on with this charade. I poured my heart out, and told them the whole business, about modeling, about Harold Wheeler, about my so-called marriage. They were quite interested in Mr. Wheeler; I provided all the information I had about him, including his address. "We'll contact you about your passport in a few days after we finish our investigation." And that was it; they dismissed us.

Now, out on the street, Mr. O'Sullivan was raring to go to the pub. "Okay, you want money? Here . . ." I reached in my bag, pulled out my last twenty pounds and handed it to him. "Now get out of my sight. I can't stand to look at you anymore."

"This is it?" Mr. O'Sullivan shook the note at me. "This is all I get?" I turned and started walking down the street. "WHORE!!" he screamed. He bent double at the waist. "YA FUCKIN" WHORE!" People walking past on the sidewalk turned to stare at me. They probably wondered why, if *I* was the whore, I was paying *him*.

In a few days immigration called and requested I come back to their office. They said they were investigating Harold Wheeler, but so far they hadn't learned much. His secretary said he'd gone to India, and it was unclear when he'd be returning. However, in the meantime, they gave me a temporary passport that was good for two months. Here was my first break in this whole ugly mess, and I vowed to make the most of those two months.

I decided to travel to Italy first, since I spoke a little of the language, having lived in a former Italian colony. True, most of my Italian consisted of Mama's cusswords, but they might come in handy. I went to Milan and loved it, doing runway work in the fashion shows. During this time I met another model, named Julie. Julie was tall, with blond shoulder-length hair and a great body; she did a lot of lingerie work. We had such a great time exploring Milan that when the shows finished there, we decided to move on and try our luck in Paris together.

These two months were fabulous for me, traveling to new places, meeting new people, eating new foods. And even though I didn't make any serious money, I still made enough to get by while I was touring Europe. Then, when the work ran out in Paris, Julie and I returned to London together.

When we got back, I met an agent from New York, who had come to England searching for new talent. He urged me to come to the States, saying he could get me lots of modeling jobs there. Of course, I was anxious for that, because everyone agreed that New York was the most lucrative market of all, especially for a black model. My agency made the arrangements, and I applied for a visa to the States.

The American Embassy reviewed my papers, then immediately contacted the British government. The upshot of that communication was a letter announcing I was being deported from England in thirty days and sent back to Somalia. In tears, I called my friend Julie, who was staying with her brother in Wales.

"I'm in trouble—big trouble. It's over for me, girl. I have to go back to Somalia."

"Oh, no, Waris. Well, why don't you come here for a few days and relax? You can take the train. It's not too far from London, and it's beautiful here. It'll do you good to get out in the country for a while, and maybe we can figure something out."

When I arrived, Julie picked me up at the station and drove through the velvet green countryside to the house. We sat down in the living room and her brother, Nigel, came in. He was short and very pale, with long fine red hair, and his front teeth and fingertips were stained with nicotine. He looked older than I expected, probably early fifties. He brought us tea on a tray, then sat there chain-smoking while I told my nightmare story of the passport dilemma, and how it was all coming to a sad end.

Leaning back in the chair with his arms folded, Nigel suddenly said, "Don't worry, I'll help you."

Shocked at this statement from a guy I'd known only about thirty minutes, I said, "How are you going to do that? How are you gonna help me?"

"I'll marry you."

I shook my head. "Oh, no. No. I've been through all that.

And that's what got me into this mess. I'm not going through that again. Enough. I can't deal with this shit. I want to go back to Africa, be happy; my family's there, and everything I know. I don't know nothing about this crazy country. Everything here is just madness and confusion. I'm going home."

Nigel jumped to his feet and ran upstairs. When he came back, he was holding up *The Sunday Times* with my picture on the cover—which had come out over a year ago, long before I ever knew Julie. "What are you doing with that?"

"I saved it because I knew one day I was going to meet you." He pointed at my eye in the photograph. "The day I saw this picture, I saw a tear here in your eye, water running down your cheek. When I looked at your face, I saw you crying and I knew you needed help. Then Allah told me—Allah said it was my duty to save you."

Oh, shit. I stared at him with my eyes open wide, thinking: *Who is this crazy motherfucker? He's the one who needs help.* But during the course of the weekend, both Nigel and Julie kept assuring me that if he could help me, why not? What future did I have back in Somalia? What was waiting for me there? My goats and camels? I asked Nigel the question that kept coming to mind: "What's in it for you, man? Why do you want to marry me, and put yourself through all this?"

"I told you—I don't want anything from you. Allah sent me to you." I explained that marrying me wasn't just a simple matter of hopping down to the registry office. I was already married.

"Well, you can divorce him, and we'll tell the government blokes we're planning to get married," Nigel reasoned, "so they won't deport you. I'll go with you. I mean, I'm a British citizen—they can't say no. Look, I feel bad for you and I'm here to help. I'll do whatever I can."

"Well, thank you very much . . ."

Julie added, "Look, if he can help you, Waris, might as well. You might as well take a chance, because what else have you got?" After listening to them for days, I decided at least she was my friend, and he was her brother. I knew where he lived, and could trust him. She was right: might as well take a chance.

We concocted a plan where Nigel would come with me to talk to Mr. O'Sullivan about a divorce, since I certainly didn't want to run into his boys again alone. I figured—as usual with everything concerning this old man—he'd want some money before he'd consent to do anything. I sighed; just thinking about it made me tired. But my friend and her brother kept urging me on, and I began to feel more optimistic about the whole plan. "Let's go," Nigel said. "We'll drive down to Croydon tomorrow."

The next day the two of us drove to the old man's neighborhood, and I gave Nigel directions to the flat. "Watch yourself," I warned as we drove. "These guys—his sons—are crazy. I mean, I'm scared to get out of the car." Nigel laughed. "I'm serious. They chased me and tried to beat me—they're mad, I tell you. We've got to be really careful."

"Come on, Waris. We'll just tell the old guy you're getting a divorce. And that's that. It's no big deal."

By the time we reached Mr. O'Sullivan's house, it was late afternoon and we parked out front on the street. As Nigel knocked on the door, I constantly looked over my shoulder up and down the street. No one answered, but I wasn't surprised. I figured we'd have to make another trip to the corner pub.

Nigel said, "Come on, let's go around and look in the window, and see if he's home." Unlike me, he was tall enough to look inside easily. But after walking to several windows without any success, he looked at me with a confused expression on his face. "I feel like something's wrong." I thought, *Oh boy, now you're getting the picture. I get that feeling every time I have anything to do with this creep.*

"What do you mean 'something's wrong'?"

"I don't know . . . I just feel . . . maybe if I can get in through this window'—and with that statement he started pounding one of the windows with the palm of his hand in order to open it.

The next-door neighbor came out and yelled, "If you're looking for Mr. O'Sullivan, we haven't seen him for weeks." As she stood there watching us with her arms folded over her apron, Nigel banged the window open a crack, and a horrid smell rushed out. I covered my mouth and nose with both hands and turned away. Nigel put his eyes down to the level of the crack and peered in. "He's dead—I can see him lying there on the floor."

We told the neighbor lady to call an ambulance, jumped in the car, and took off. I hate to say it, but all I felt was relief.

Shortly after we discovered Mr. O'Sullivan rotting in his kitchen, Nigel and I were married. The British government stopped proceedings to deport me, but made no secret of the fact they thought our marriage was a crock. And, of course, it was. Still, Nigel and I agreed that until I got my passport, it would be best for me to stay at his place in Wales.

After living first in Mogadishu, then London, for seven years, I'd forgotten how much I enjoyed nature. And even though the leafy-green countryside scattered with farmland and rivers was completely different from the deserts of Somalia, I enjoyed spending time outside again as opposed to being in high-rise buildings and windowless studios. In Wales I was able to resume some of my favorite pleasures from my nomad days: running, walking, picking wildflowers, and peeing outside. Occasionally someone would catch me with my ass poking out of the shrubbery.

Nigel and I had separate rooms and lived like roommates— not husband and wife. We had made an agreement that he would marry me so that I could get my passport, and although I offered to help him financially when I started making money, he insisted he expected nothing in return. Nigel only wanted the joy received from following Allah's advice to help another human being in need. One morning I got up earlier than usual, around six, because I was headed to London for a casting. I came downstairs and put the coffee on while Nigel remained asleep in his room. I had just pulled my yellow rubber gloves on and begun washing the dishes when the doorbell rang.

Still wearing my gloves dripping soapsuds, I opened the door and found two men standing there. They wore gray suits and serious gray faces, and carried black briefcases. "Mrs. Richards?"

"Yes?"

"Is your husband here?"

"Yes, he's upstairs."

"Step out of the way, please. We're here on official government business." As if anybody else would walk around looking like that.

"Well, come in, come in—hey, you want a coffee or something? Sit down, and I'll get him." They sat down in Nigel's big comfortable living room chairs, but didn't permit their backs to rest against the furniture. "Oh, darling," I called sweetly. "Come downstairs, please. We have some visitors here."

He came down still half asleep, his blond hair tangled. "Hello." Nigel knew immediately by the way they looked who they were. "Yes, can I help you?"

"Well, yes, we'd just like to ask you a couple of questions. First of all, we want to make sure you and your wife live together. Do you live together?"

I could see from the look of pure disgust on Nigel's face that things were going to get interesting and leaned up against the wall to watch. He spat out, "Well, what does it look like to you now?"

The two agents looked nervously around the room. "Umm. Yes, sir. We believe you, but we still need to have a look around the house."

Nigel's face grew dark, ominous, like a storm cloud. "Look.

You're not going through my house. I don't care who you are. This is my wife, we live together, you see how it is. You came in unannounced—we didn't dress up for you—so get out of my house!"

"Mr. Richards, you don't have to get so angry. By law we're required to—"

"YOU MAKE ME SICK!!!" *Run, boys, run while you can.* Instead, they just sat there glued to their chairs with looks of astonishment on their pasty faces. "GET OUT OF MY HOUSE! If you ever come around here or call me again, I'm gonna get my gun, I'm gonna fuckin' shoot you, and I'll—I'll die for her," he said, pointing at me.

I just shook my head, thinking. *This guy is crazy. He is really, really falling for me, and I'm in deep trouble. What in the hell am I doing here? I should have gone back to Africa—I would have been better off.* After living there a couple of months, I was saying, "Nigel, why don't you clean yourself up, get some decent shoes, and get a girlfriend? Let me help you."

And he would respond, "Girlfriend? I don't want a girlfriend. For God's sake, I have a wife—what would I want with a girlfriend?"

When he would say this, I would go berserk. "Go put your fucking head in the toilet, you psycho, and flush it! Man, wake up and get out of my life! I don't *love* you! You and I made an agreement—you wanted to help me—but I can't be what you want me to be. I can't pretend I love you just to make you happy." But even though Nigel and I had made an agreement, he broke it and made his own. When he was screaming himself purple at the agents who visited his house, he wasn't lying. In his mind, every word of it was true. And things became even more complicated because I depended on him, liked him as a friend, was grateful to him for helping me, wanted no part of him romantically, and seriously wanted to kill him when he started acting like I was his beloved wife and personal property. Quickly I realized I had to get away, and the sooner the better.

But the passport dilemma dragged on. As Nigel realized I was dependent on him, the sense of power drove him to be more and more demanding. He became obsessed with me—where I was, what I was doing, whom I was with. He constantly pleaded for me to love him, and the more he begged, the more I loathed him. Sometimes I would get jobs in London, or go to visit friends. I took every chance to get away from Nigel in an attempt to remain sane.

However, I was losing my ability to remain sane while I was living with a man who I thought was insane. I grew tired of waiting for my passport—my ticket to freedom—and one day, heading to London, I stood on the platform wanting desperately to throw myself in front of the oncoming train. In those few minutes, I listened to its roar, felt the cold wind of its force blow my hair, and thought about what those tons of steel would feel like as they crushed my bones. The temptation to end all my worries was strong, but finally I asked myself: *Why waste my life because of this man?*

To his credit, after waiting for over a year, Nigel went to the immigration office and created a spectacular scene that finally got them to issue me a temporary passport. He cried, "My wife is an international model, and she needs at least a temporary passport so she can travel for her career." BAM! He slammed my portfolio of modeling shots down on the desk. "I am a fucking British citizen, and for you to treat my wife like this— well, I'm appalled, I'm ashamed to say this is my country. I demand this be sorted out NOW!" Shortly after his visit, the government confiscated my old Somalian passport, and sent me a temporary travel document that permitted me to leave the country but had to be constantly renewed. Stamped inside were the words: "Good for travel anywhere except Somalia." They were the most depressing words I could imagine. Somalia was at war, and England didn. want to take a chance on my visiting a nation at war while I was under its care. As a British resident, they would be responsible for me. As I read the words "Good for travel anywhere except Somalia," I whispered, "Oh, my God, what have I done? I can't even go to my own country." Now I was completely alien.

Had anyone told me what my options were, I would have said forget it, give me back my Somalian passport. But no one discussed it with me. And now it was too late to go back. Since I couldn't go back, there was only one direction to go and that was forward. I applied for a visa to America, and booked a flight to New York—alone.

14.

THE BIG LEAGUE

Nigel kept insisting that he had to come to New York with me. He'd never been there before, yet he knew all about the city: "That place is totally crazy. And you, Waris—you don't know what you're doing, where you're going—you'll be completely lost without me. And it's not safe for you to be there alone—I'm going to protect you." Yeah, but who was going to protect me from Nigel? One of his more endearing traits was that in an argument, he would repeat his warped logic—over and over and over and over and over . . . like a crazy parrot, until he wore you down, no matter what you said to him. There was no reasoning with him. But I was not giving in this time. I looked at this trip as a big opportunity for my future, not only for my career, but as a fresh start, away from Britain, away from Nigel and our whole sick relationship.

In 1991, I arrived in the States alone, and the booker at my New York agency gave me his apartment while he stayed at a friend's. The apartment was in the Village, right in the heart of everything exciting in Manhattan. There wasn't much in the studio except a big bed, but that simplicity suited me fine.

My agency had lots of jobs lined up for me when I got there, and I immediately began running in a way I never had before, and making money in a way I never had before. I worked every day that first week I arrived. After having struggled for four years to get work, I wasn't complaining.

Everything was going great until one afternoon when I was on a shoot. During a break, I called the agency to check on the next day's appointments. My booker said, "And your husband called. He's on his way and will meet you at the apartment tonight."

"My husband—you gave him the address where I'm staying?"

"Uh-huh. He said you were so frantic before you left, you forgot to give it to him. Your husband was so cute, he said, 'I just want to make sure she's all right, because, you know, it's her first time in New York.'" I slammed down the receiver and stood there for a minute breathing hard. I couldn't believe it. Yes, I could, but still he had gone too far this time. I didn't blame this poor guy at the agency; he had no idea that Nigel wasn't a *real* husband. And how could I explain it to him? *See, we're married and everything, but I just married him for his passport because I was an illegal alien then and they were deporting me to Somalia. Got it? Now, about those appointments for tomorrow*— The scariest part was that I really *was* legally married to him.

When I finished work, I came back to the apartment that evening, with my mind made up. As I'd been forewarned, Nigel arrived and knocked on the door. I let him in, and before he could take his jacket off, I said in a deadly, no-nonsense tone, "Come on, let's go. I'll take you out for dinner." Once we were safely seated in public, I spelled it out for him: "Look, Nigel, I can't stand you. *I can't stand you.* You make me sick! I can't work when you're around me. I can't think. I'm frustrated. I'm tense, and I just want you to go away." I knew what I was saying to him was horrible, and it gave me no pleasure to hurt him. But I was desperate. Maybe if I was cruel enough, mean enough, I could finally get through to him.

He looked so sad and pathetic that I felt guilty. "Okay, you've made your point. I shouldn't have come. I'll take the first flight home tomorrow."

"Good! Go! I don't want to see you in that apartment when I get home from the studio. I'm working here—this isn't a holiday. I don't have time for your craziness." But when I got home the next evening, he hadn't budged. He was sitting there looking out the window of the dark apartment—listless, lonely, miserable—but there all the same. When I started screaming, he agreed to go the next day. And the next. Finally he left and went back to Wales, and I thought: *Thank you, God; finally I can have some peace*. My stay in New York lengthened as the work continued to pour in. However, Nigel didn't permit me any peace for long. He flew back to New York again twice more, three times in all, each time showing up unannounced.

In spite of the absurd situation with Nigel, everything else in my life was heavenly. I was having a great time meeting people in New York, and my career took off like a rocket. I worked for Benetton and Levi's, and appeared in a series of commercials for a jeweler, Pomellato, wearing white African robes. I did makeup ads for Revlon, then later represented their new perfume, Ajee. The commercial announced: "From the heart of Africa comes a fragrance to capture the heart of every woman." These companies were utilizing the thing that made me different—my exotic African look, the same look that had kept me from getting modeling jobs in London. For the Academy Awards, Revlon filmed a special commercial where I appeared with Cindy Crawford, Claudia Schiffer, and Lauren Hutton. In this spot, each of us kept asking and answering the same question: "What makes a woman revolutionary?" My answer summed up the bizarre reality of my life: "A nomad from Somalia becoming a Revlon model."

Later, I became the first black model ever to be featured in ads for Oil of Olay. I made music videos for Robert Palmer and Meat Loaf. These projects kept snowballing and soon I was in the big fashion magazines: *Elle*, *Allure*, *Glamour*, Italian *Vogue*, French *Vogue*. Along the way, I got to work with the biggest photographers in the business, including the legendary Richard Avedon. In spite of the fact that he's more famous than the models he photographs, I loved Richard because he's so down-to-earth and funny. And even though he's been doing this for decades, he would constantly ask my opinion about shots: "Waris, what do you think about this?" The fact that he cared enough to ask meant a lot to me. Richard joined my first great photographer, Terence Donovan, as a man I respected.

Through the years, I've developed a list of favorite photo-graphers. It sounds easy to have a job taking pictures all day, but after I became more experienced, I started to see a huge difference in quality, at least from my perspective of being the subject of those photographs. A great fashion photographer is one who is able to bring out the true individuality of the model and enhance it, instead of imposing a preconceived image on her. Part of my appreciation may be that as I get older, I appreciate more who I am and what makes me different from the women I constantly work with in the modeling business. To be a black in this industry, where everybody's six feet tall and has silky hair down to her knees and porcelain-white skin, is to be an exception. And I've worked with photographers who used lighting and makeup and hair stylists to make me look like something I wasn't. But I didn't enjoy it, and I didn't like the end result. If you want Cindy Crawford, you should definitely use Cindy, instead of taking a black woman and slapping a long wig and a bunch of light foundation on her to make a weird, black Cindy Crawford look-alike. The photographers I enjoyed working with appreciated the natural beauty in women and tried to seek out that beauty. In my case, they no doubt had their work cut out for them, but I respected the effort.

As my popularity grew, my commitments grew, and my schedule was packed with castings, shows, and shoots. All of it was very difficult for me to keep track of, with my bias against wearing a watch. I discovered problems trying to tell time the old way; it was tough to observe the length of my shadow amidst Manhattan skyscrapers. I started to get in a lot of trouble for showing up late for appointments. I also discovered that I was dyslexic when I kept showing up at the wrong address. My agency would write down the address for me, and I would always reverse the numbers. They'd give me an address, 725 Broadway, and I'd show up at 527 Broadway wondering what happened to everybody. I had done this in London, too, but since I was working so much more in New York, I began to realize this was a constant problem.

As I became more experienced and confident in my career, my favorite part of modeling emerged: the runway. Twice a year, the designers hold shows to announce their new line. The circuit for the fashion shows begins in Milan and lasts for two weeks. Next it's on to Paris, then London, then New York. My nomad days prepared me well for this life: traveling light, moving on when the work did, accepting what life had to offer and making the most of it.

When the shows begin in Milan for the season, every woman and girl in modeling heads there, along with every woman and girl who's ever dreamed of becoming a model. Suddenly the city is mobbed by extremely tall mutant women, running everywhere like ants. You will see them on every street corner, at every bus stop, in every café—models. *Oh, there's one now. There's another one. Yes, there's one.* There's no mistaking the look. Some are friendly. "Hi!" Some just look each other up and down. "Um-hmmm." Some know each other. Some are complete strangers, there for the first time all alone and scared to death. Some get along. Some don't. There are all kinds, all types. And anybody who says there's no jealousy, well, that's complete bullshit. There's plenty of that going on, too.

The agency sets up your appointments, then the models run around Milan going to castings, trying to secure a spot in the shows. This is when you realize that modeling is not all about glamour. Hardly. You might have seven, ten, eleven appointments in a single day. And it's very, very hard work, because you're running around all day; you don't have time to eat because you have one appointment and are late for two others. When you finally make it to your next casting, thirty girls are lined up waiting. And you know that every single one of them has to go before you do. When it's your turn, you show your book—your portfolio with your photographs. If the client likes you, he'll ask you to walk. And if he really likes you, he'll ask you to try something on. Then that's it: "Thank you very much. Next!"

You don't know if you made it or not, but you don't have time to worry about it, because you're on to the next one. If they're interested, they contact your agency and book you. Meanwhile, you better learn quickly not to dwell on the job, or get upset about losing jobs you really wanted, or feel hurt being rejected by your favorite designers. When you start thinking, *Oh, did I get it? Am I going to get it? Why didn't I get it?* you drive yourself absolutely crazy, especially when you're turned down for assignments. If you let it bother you, you'll soon start falling to pieces. Eventually you realize the whole casting process is mostly about disappointment. In the beginning, I used to worry, *Well, why didn't I get that one? Damn, I really wanted that job!* But I later learned to live by my motto with this business: *C'est la vie.* Well, shit, *it just didn't work.* They didn't like you, simple as that. And it's not your fault. If they were looking for somebody seven feet tall with long blond hair who weighs eighty pounds, well, they're not interested in Waris. Just move on, girl.

———

If a client books you, you go back and do the fitting for the clothes you'll wear in the show. All this activity is going on, and we haven't even gotten to the show yet. You're getting rundown and exhausted, and you haven't slept well, and you don't have time to eat right. You're looking tired and skinny. And then skinnier and skinnier, while every day you're fighting to look your best, because your career depends on it. Then you're wondering, Why am I doing this? Why am I here?

When the fashion shows begin, sometimes you're still doing castings at the same time, because the whole process only lasts two weeks. On the day of the show, you have to be there about five hours before it begins. All the girls are packed in, you get your makeup done, then you sit around, then you get your hair done, then you sit around waiting for the show to start. Next, you put your first outfit on, then you stand around, because you can't sit down and wrinkle the clothes! And when the show starts, suddenly it's chaos—complete madness. "Whoa! Where are you? What are you doing? Where's Waris? Where's Naomi? Come here. Come front—hurry up. You're number nine. You're next." You jerk your clothes on in front of all these strange people you don't know. "Ah, ah, I'm coming, yeah— hold on." Everybody's pushing everybody. "What are you doing? Get out of my way—I'm on!"

And then, after all that hard work is the best little bit: you're on. You're next, standing off stage. Then BOOM! You walk out on the runway, and the lights are blazing, and the music's blasting, and everybody's staring, and you're sashaying down the walk for all you're worth, thinking, *I AM IT. ALL OF YOU—LOOK AT ME!* You've had your hair and makeup done by the best in the business, and you're wearing an outfit that's so expensive you could never dream of buying it. But for a few seconds it's yours, and you know you look like a million bucks. The rush shoots through you, and when you leave the runway, you can't wait to change and get back out there again. After all that preparation, the whole show lasts only twenty or thirty minutes, but you may do three, four, five shows in a day, so you have to tear out and head to your next one as soon as you're finished.

When the two weeks of insanity is finished in Milan, the colony of designers, makeup artists, hairstylists, and models moves on to Paris like a band of gypsies. Then the whole process repeats itself, before they go on to London and New York. By the end of the circuit, you're barely hanging on, and when you finish in New York, you better take some time off. You're ready to go to some little island somewhere with no telephones to try and relax. Otherwise, if you don't, if you try to keep working, you'll go absolutely mental from being worn out.

While modeling is fun—and I admit to loving the glamour and glitter and beauty of it—there's a cruel side that can be devastating for a woman, especially a young one, who's insecure. I've gone in for jobs and had the stylist or photographer exclaim in horror: "My God! What is wrong with your feet! Why do you have those ugly black marks all over them?" What can I say? They're referring to the scars caused by stepping on hundreds of thorns and rocks in the Somalian desert; a reminder of my childhood, when I walked for fourteen years with no shoes. How can I explain that to a designer in Paris?

When they'd ask me to try on a miniskirt at a casting, I'd immediately feel sick. I'd walk out and stand on one foot, twisting around, hoping they wouldn't notice my problem. I've got bowlegs—the legacy of growing up in a nomadic family without proper nutrition. And I've been fired from jobs because of these bowlegs, a physical ailment I had no control over.

I used to be so ashamed, so hurt, because of my legs that I once went to a doctor to see if he could fix them. "Break my legs," I ordered him, "so I won't have to feel humiliated anymore." But thank God, he said I was too old, the bones were already set, and it wouldn't work. As I got older, I thought,

Well, these are my legs, and they're a result of who I am and where I'm from. And as I got to know my body better, I came to love my legs. If I had broken them so that I could do some runway show for five minutes, I would be very, very angry with myself today. I would have broken my limbs for what—so I could make some guy's clothes look good? Now I'm proud of these legs because they have history; they're part of the history of my life. My bowlegs carried me thousands of miles across the desert and my slow, undulating walk is the walk of an African woman; it speaks of my heritage.

Another problem with modeling is that the fashion business, like any other industry, has its share of unpleasant people. Maybe because so much is at stake in some of the decisions, people let the stress get to them. But I remember working with a particular art director at one of the major fashion magazines, who—for me—epitomized the bitter, bitchy attitude that made a photo shoot feel like a funeral. We were in the Caribbean, shooting on a beautiful little island. This place was like paradise, and all of us should have been having a great time, since we were getting paid to work in a setting most people would pay dearly to visit for a holiday. But not this woman. From the minute we arrived she was on my back. "Waris, you really need to get yourself together. You need to get up and get moving—you're just lazy. I can't stand working with people like you." She called the agency back in New York and complained that I was just a moron and refused to do any work. They were quite mystified, but no more so than I was.

This art director was a heartbreakingly sad woman. She was obviously frustrated, she didn't have a man, no friends, nobody to love. And all her life, love, and passion were poured into this business because she had nothing else going for her. So she took all her frustration out on me, and I'm sure I wasn't the first one—or the last. After a few days of this, however, I lost my sympathy for her. I looked at her and I thought, *There are two things I can do to this one: I can slap her across the face, or I can just look at her and smile and say nothing.* And I thought: *It's best to say nothing.*

The saddest thing is to see a woman like this art director get hold of young girls who're just starting out in the business. Sometimes these girls, who are no more than children, leave Oklahoma or Georgia or North Dakota and fly to New York or France or Italy alone and try to make it. Often they don't know the country or the language. They're naive and get taken advantage of. They can't deal with the rejection and fall apart. They don't have the experience or wisdom or inner strength to realize the fault doesn't lie with them. Many wind up coming back home sobbing, broken and bitter.

Crooks and con artists also abound in this business. Many young girls want desperately to be models, and they fall into these scams where a so-called agency charges them a fortune to put a portfolio together. Having been a victim of this type of thief when I met up with Harold Wheeler, this outrages me. Modeling is about making money, not paying money. If a person wants to be a model, the only money she needs is bus fare to visit the agencies. She can look in the Yellow Pages, call up, and make an appointment for a visit. And if the agency starts talking about fees—she should run! If a legitimate agency thinks someone has the right look, the look for the times, they'll help her put together a book. And then, they'll book her appointments and castings, and she's working.

If some of the people in modeling are unpleasant, some of the conditions are not always the best either. I accepted one project that I knew involved a bull, but until I had flown from New York to Los Angeles, then taken a helicopter into the desert, I didn't know exactly how much bull.

We were completely isolated in the California desert, just me, the crew, and a monstrous black bull with long pointy horns. I went into the little trailer and had my hair and makeup done. When I finished, the photographer led me outside to this animal. "Say hello to Satan," he said.

"Ohhh, hello, Satan." I loved him. "He's beautiful. Fantastic. But, is he safe?"

"Oh, yeah, of course. This is the owner." The photographer pointed at a man holding Satan's lead. "He knows what to do." The photographer explained the project to me. The shot would appear on a liquor bottle label. I would be sitting on top of the bull. Naked. This news was a big shock indeed, because I'd had no idea about any of this before I arrived. But I didn't want to make a big fuss in front of all these people, so I figured I might as well get it over with.

I felt sorry for the bull because it was miserably hot in the desert, and his nose was dripping. All his feet were manacled in position so he couldn't move, and this huge beast stood there humbly. The photographer put his hands down to act as a step to boost me up on the bull's back. "Lie down," he commanded, waving his arm. "Stretch out across the bull—put your upper body down across the bull and stretch your legs out." The whole time I was trying to look beautiful and relaxed and playful and sexy, I was thinking: *If this thing bucks me off, I'm dead*. Suddenly I felt his furry back flex beneath my naked belly, and I saw the landscape of the Mojave fly by as I sailed through the air and hit the baked dirt with a thud.

"Are you all right?"

"Yeah, yeah." I was playing tough now, trying not to act shook up. I didn't want anybody to call Waris Dirie a coward—afraid of an old bull. "Yeah, let's go. Help me back on top again." The crew picked me up and dusted me off, and we started again. Evidently the bull was not enjoying the heat, because he bucked me off twice more. On the third landing I sprained my ankle, which began to swell and throb immediately. "Well, did you get the shot?" I called from the ground.

"Oh, it would be beautiful if we could get one more roll . . ."

Fortunately, that bull shot never appeared. For some reason they never used it, and I was glad. The thought of a bunch of old men sitting around drinking liquor and looking at my naked butt was very sad. After this project, I decided not to do any more nude shots, because I simply didn't like it. The money was not worth the feeling of being vulnerable, standing there in front of people feeling completely awkward and helpless, waiting for a break when I could run grab my towel.

Although the bull job was probably my worst, most of the time when I'm modeling, I love it; it's the most fun career anybody could ask for. I could never get used to the idea, from the time Terence Donovan took me to Bath and stood me in front of a camera, that anybody would pay me simply for the way I looked. I never really thought that I'd be able to make a living from something that seemed so little like work. Instead the whole business just seemed like a silly game to me, but I'm glad I stuck it out. I've always felt grateful that I got the opportunity to succeed in this business, because not every girl can get that break. Sadly, so many young girls try so hard, and often it just doesn't work out.

I remember when I was young, working as Uncle Mohammed's maid, and dreaming of being a model. And that night I finally worked up the courage to ask Iman how to get started. Ten years later, I was working on a Revlon shoot in a New York studio when the makeup artist came in and said Iman was next door photographing her new line of cosmetics. I rushed out and went to see her. "Oh, I see now you're doing your own product line. Why didn't you use me, a Somali woman, to pose in the ads for your makeup?" I asked.

She looked at me defensively and mumbled, "Well, I can't afford you."

I said to her in Somali, "*I would have done it for you for free.*" Funny, she has never realized that I'm the same little girl, the maid, who used to bring her tea.

The odd fact is that I never went in search of modeling, it came to me; maybe that's why I never took it too seriously. The thrill didn't lie in being a "supermodel" or a "star," because I still can't understand why models have become so famous. Each day, I watch the whole fashion scene become more and more frantic with magazines and TV shows about supermodels, and I wonder: *What is it all about?*

Simply because we're models, some people treat us like goddesses and some people treat us like idiots. I've run into this last attitude plenty of times. It's as if because I make my living with my face, I must be stupid. With a smug expression, people say, "You're a model? Oh, too bad—no brains at all. All you have to do is just stand there and look pretty for the camera."

However, I've met all types of models, and yes, I've met some who were not very bright. But the majority are intelligent, sophisticated, well traveled, and as knowledgeable about most subjects as any other worldly person. They know how to handle themselves and their business, and act completely professional. For people like that insecure bitchy art director, it's tough to handle the fact that some women can be beautiful *and* smart. So there's a need to put us in our place by talking down to us, as if we're just a flock of gawky dimpled dimwits.

I find the moral issues surrounding modeling and advertising incredibly complicated. I believe the most important priorities in the world are nature, personal goodness, family, and friendship. Yet I make my living by saying, "Buy this because it looks beautiful." I'm selling stuff with a big smile. I could be cynical about it all and say, "Why am I doing this? I'm helping destroy the world." But I believe almost anybody in any career could say that about their work at some point. The good that comes from what I do is that I've met beautiful people and seen beautiful places and experienced different cultures that have made me want to do something to help the world instead of destroy it. And instead of being another poverty-stricken Somali, I'm in a position to do something about it.

Instead of wanting to be a star or celebrity, I've enjoyed modeling mostly because I felt like a citizen of the world, and was able to travel to some of the most phenomenal places on the planet. Many times when I was traveling for work, we'd go to some beautiful island and I would escape to the beach every chance I got and just run. It felt so wonderful to be free in nature, back in the sun again. Then I would sneak off into the trees and sit quietly and just listen to the birds singing. Ahhh. I would close my eyes, smell the sweetness of the flowers, feel the sun on my face, listen to the birds, and pretend I was back in Africa. I would try to recapture that feeling of peace and tranquillity I remember from Somalia, and pretend I was back home again.

15.

BACK TO SOMALIA

In 1995, after a long stretch of photo shoots and fashion shows, I escaped to Trinidad to relax. It was Carnival time and everyone was in costume, dancing and rejoicing, reveling in the sheer joy of life. I was staying at the home of a family I knew; I'd been there a couple of days when a man came to their door. The matriarch of the family, an elderly woman we called Auntie Monica, went to answer the door. It was late afternoon, and the sun was hot outside, but the room where we sat was cool and shady. The man standing at the door was in silhouette against the bright light; I couldn't see him, but I heard him say he was looking for somebody named Waris. Then Auntie Monica called, "Waris, you have a phone call."

"Phone call? Where is the phone?"

"You have to go with this man. He'll take you there."

I followed him back to his place. He was a neighbor of Auntie Monica's who lived a few doors away and was the only person in the area with a telephone. We walked through his living room to the hall where he pointed to a receiver lying off the hook. "Hello?" It was my agency in London.

"Oh, hello, Waris. Sorry to trouble you, but we've been contacted by the BBC. They say it's urgent you get in touch with them right away. They want to talk to you about making a documentary."

"Documentary about what?"

"About being a supermodel, and where you came from and, you know, how does it feel living your new life."

"That's not a story. I mean, for goodness sake, can't they find something better?"

"Well, anyway, you talk to them about it. What time should I tell them you'll call?"

"Look, I don't want to talk to anybody."

"But they really want to talk to you right away."

"Hey, whatever. Just tell them I'll talk to them when I get to London. I have to go back to New York when I leave here, then fly to London. I'll call them when I get there."

"All right, then. I'll tell them."

But the next day, while I was out carousing around town, the man came back to Auntie Monica's again, saying there was another phone call for Waris. I completely ignored this news. Again, the next day, another phone call. This time I went back with the gentleman, because obviously they were going to wear him out running over to get me. Of course, it was my agency again. "Yeah, what is it?"

"Yes, Waris, it's the BBC again. They say it's very urgent they talk to you; they're going to call you tomorrow at this same time."

"Look, it's my break time, okay? No way I'm talking to anybody. I've escaped from all that, so leave me alone and quit bothering this poor man."

"They just want to ask you a couple of questions."

I sighed. "For God's sake. All right. Tell them to call me tomorrow at this number." The next day I spoke with the director, Gerry Pomeroy, who makes films for the BBC. He asked me questions about my life.

I replied curtly: "First of all, I don't want to talk about this now. I'm supposed to be here on holiday. You know? Can't we talk another time?"

"I'm sorry, but we have to make a decision, and I need some information." So I stood in a stranger's hallway in Trinidad, telling the story of my life to a stranger in London. "Okay, great, Waris. We'll get back to you."

Two days later the man came to Auntie Monica's again. "Phone call for Waris." I shrugged at him, shook my head, and followed him down the street. It was Gerry from the BBC. "Yes, Waris, we really want to do a documentary of your life. It will be a half-hour episode for a show called *The Day That Changed My Life*.

In the meantime, between the first phone call from my agency and the second call from the BBC, I'd been thinking about all this documentary business. "Well, listen, uh, Gerry— I'll make a deal with you. I'll do this with you guys if you take me back to Somalia and help me find my mother." He agreed, thinking my return to Africa would make a good conclusion to the story. Gerry told me to call him as soon as I got back to London; then we'd sit down and plan the whole project.

Returning with the BBC would be the first opportunity I'd had to go home since I left Mogadishu, because of my myriad passport problems, tribal wars in Somalia, and my inability to locate my family. Even if I'd been able to fly to Mogadishu, it wasn't exactly as if I could call my mother and tell her to meet me at the airport. From the moment the BBC promised to take me, I could think of nothing else. I had numerous meetings with Gerry and his assistant, Colm, to plan the project and elaborate on the story of my life.

We started filming in London right away. I returned to all my old haunts starting with Uncle Mohammed's house—the Somalian ambassador's residence—which the BBC got permission to enter. They filmed All Souls Church School, where I was discovered by Malcolm Fairchild. Later they interviewed him on camera, asking why he was so interested in photographing an unknown servant. The crew filmed me doing a photo shoot with Terence Donovan. They interviewed my good friend Sarah Doukas, the director of Storm, a London modeling agency.

The heat on the whole project was turned up considerably when the BBC decided to follow me on a gig hosting *Soul Train*, a TV program that features the best in black music. I had never done a project like this before and was a complete nervous wreck. Added to that was the problem that when we got to L.A., I had a terrible cold and could barely talk. And the whole time I was traveling from London to Los Angeles, blowing my nose, reading my script, getting ready for the show, riding in the limo, I was being filmed by my constant shadows: the BBC film crew. The insanity was multiplied when we went to the studio and the BBC documentary crew was filming the *Soul Train* crew filming me. And if there was ever an act that I didn't want to have documented, this had to be the one. I'm sure I was the worst host in the history of *Soul Train*, but Don Cornelius and the production crew were so patient with me. We started at ten in the morning and worked till nine that night. I think it was their longest day ever. My old difficulty with reading still plagued me, as it had in my James Bond film debut. Although my skill was much improved, I still struggled reading aloud. And trying to read from cue cards in front of two film crews, dozens of dancers, and a handful of internationally famous singers, while lights blazed in my eyes, was more of a challenge than I was up for. They were screaming, "Take twenty-six . . . Cut!" "Take seventy-six . . . Cut!" The music would start playing, dancers would start dancing, and everybody would start filming, then I'd bungle my lines: "Take ninety-six . . . Cut!" The dancers would freeze, then let their arms flop down to their sides and glare at me as if saying, "Who *is* this stupid bitch? Oh, God, where did you find her? We just want to go home."

My host's duties included welcoming Donna Summer, which was a big honor for me, because she's one of my all-time favorite singers. "Ladies and gentlemen, please put your hands together and welcome the lady of soul, Donna Summer!"

"CUT!!"

"WHAT NOW?"

"You forgot to say her label. Read the cue card, Waris."

"Ohhhh, Fucking-A! Will you pick this shit up, pick it up? I can't see it. And don't put it down. Put it up straight—these lights are right in my eyes. I can't see a thing."

Don Cornelius would take me into the corner and say, "Take a deep breath. Tell me how you're feeling." I explained to him that this script just wasn't working for me—it wasn't my groove—the way I speak.

"How do you want to do it? Go ahead. Take over—take it all." They were amazingly patient and calm. Don and the crew let me take over and make a mess out of everything, then helped me fix it up again. The best part of that whole experience was working with them and Donna Summer, who gave me an autographed CD of her greatest hits.

Then the BBC and I moved on to New York. They followed me out to do a job on location where I was being photographed in the rain, walking up and down the streets of Manhattan—wearing a black slip and a raincoat and holding an umbrella. On another night, the cameraman sat quietly in the corner filming while I cooked dinner with a group of friends at an apartment in Harlem. We were having such a good time that we forgot he was there.

The next phase required me and the whole crew to meet in London and fly to Africa, where I would reunite with my family for the first time since I'd run away. While we were filming in London, Los Angeles, and New York, the BBC staff in Africa began searching diligently for my mother. In order to locate my family, we went over maps, and I tried to show them the regions where we usually traveled. Next, I had to go over all the tribal and clan names of my family, which is very confusing, especially for Westerners. For the past three months the BBC had been searching—without success.

The plan was that I would remain in New York working until the BBC found Mama, then I'd fly to London, and we'd all go to Africa together and film the conclusion of my story. Shortly after the BBC began looking for Mama, Gerry called one day and said, "We found your mother."

"Oh, wonderful!"

"Well, we think we found her."

I said, "What do you mean 'you think'?"

"Okay, we found this woman, and we asked her if she had a daughter named Waris. She said, yes, yes, she has a daughter named Waris. Yes, Waris lives in London. But she seems awfully vague on the details, so our people in Somalia aren't sure what's going on—if this woman is the mother of another Waris or what." After further questioning, the BBC disqualified this woman, but the search was just beginning. Suddenly the desert was alive with women claiming to be my mother; they all had daughters named Waris who lived in London, which was especially odd, considering I have never met another human being with my name.

I explained what was going on. "See, these people are so poor over there, they're desperate. They're hoping if they say 'Yeah, we're her family,' you'll come to their little village and make a film, and they can get some money, get some food. These women are pretending to be my mother, hoping they'll get something out of it. I don't know how they think they're gonna get away with it, but they'll try."

Unfortunately, I had no pictures of my mother, but Gerry came up with another idea. "We need some kind of secret that only your mother would know about you."

"Well, my mother used to have a nickname for me, Avdohol, which means small mouth."

"Will she remember that?"

"Absolutely."

From then on, Avdohol became the secret password. When the BBC was interviewing, these women would make it through the first couple of questions; then they'd always flunk out on the nickname. Bye-bye. But finally one day they called me and said, "We think we've found her. This woman didn't remember the nickname, but she said she has a daughter named Waris who used to work for the ambassador in London."

I hopped a flight out of New York the next day. When I got to London, the BBC needed a few more days to make preparations. We would take a flight to Addis Ababa in Ethiopia, then charter a small plane to take us to the Ethiopia-Somalia border. The trip would be very dangerous. We couldn't go into Somalia because of the war, so my family would have to come across the border to us. The place where we were landing was in the middle of the desert; there was no landing strip, just rocks and brush.

While the BBC was getting ready for the trip, I stayed in a hotel in London. Nigel came to visit me. I tried to remain on cordial terms with him because of my precarious circumstances. By this time, I was paying the mortgage on his house in Wales, because he had no job and refused to look for one. I even got him a job working for some people I knew but they fired him after three weeks, and told him not to come around again. From the beginning, when Nigel first learned of the documentary, he started pestering me to go to Africa with us. "I want to come. I want to make sure you're all right."

I said, "NO, you are not coming. How am I supposed to explain you to my mother? Who are you supposed to be?"

"Well, I'm your husband!"

"No, you're not! Forget it. All right? Just forget about it." One thing was for sure, he was not the type of person I wanted to introduce to my mother. Certainly not as my husband.

Back when I was having the initial planning sessions with the BBC, Nigel had insisted on tagging along. Quickly, Gerry had enough of him. We'd usually meet up for dinner, and Gerry would call that day and say, "He's not coming with you tonight, is he? Please, Waris, let's leave him out of this."

When I came back to London, Nigel came to my hotel and started in again on his campaign to come to Africa. When I refused, he stole my passport. Of course, he knew that in a few days, we were supposed to leave the country. Nothing I said could persuade him to give it back to me. Finally, in desperation, I met Gerry one night and told him, "Gerry, you're not going to believe it. He took my passport and won't give it back to me."

Gerry put his forehead down on his hand and closed his eyes. "Oh, my God, I'm really getting fed up with this, Waris. I'm so sick of dealing with this shit, I've just—I've really had enough." Gerry and the other guys at the BBC tried reasoning with Nigel. "Look, act like a grown-up—be a man. We're almost at the end of this project; you can't do this to us. We need this story to end in Africa, which means we've got to take Waris there. Now, for God's sake, please —" But Nigel wasn't interested. He went back to Wales with my passport.

I made the trip to Wales alone and begged him. Again and again, he refused to give it to me unless he got to go to Africa with us. It was a hopeless bind for me. I'd prayed for the chance to see my mother again for fifteen years. With Nigel there, the whole experience would be ruined. No doubt about it—he'd make sure of that. If I didn't take him, I had no chance of seeing her, because I couldn't travel without my passport. "Nigel, you can't be following us around and making a bloody headache for everybody. Don't you see—it's my chance to see my mother for the first time in fifteen years!"

He was so bitter that we were going to Africa and it had nothing to do with him. "I swear, you're just being so fucking unfair!" he cried. Finally, in the end, I convinced him to give me my passport by promising I'd take him to Africa some day, when this job was done—just the two of us. It was a cheap trick, and I wasn't proud of it, because that was a promise I knew I'd never keep. But when it came to Nigel, being a decent, reasonable adult never worked.

The twin-engine bush plane landed in Galadi, Ethiopia, a tiny village where Somali refugees had gathered across the border to escape the fighting at home. As we hit the red desert soil strewn with rocks, the plane bounced wildly. You must have been able to see the trail of dust for miles, because the entire village ran toward us. They'd never seen anything like this before. The BBC crew and I all climbed out of the plane, and I began trying to speak Somali to the people hurrying to meet us. I was struggling to communicate with them, because some were Ethiopians and some were Somalis, but they spoke a different dialect. Within a few minutes I gave up.

I smelled the hot air and the sand and suddenly I remembered my lost childhood. Every little thing came flooding back to me and I began to run. The crew was yelling, "Waris, where are you going?"

"Go on . . . go wherever you have to go . . . I'll be back." I ran and touched the ground and rubbed the earth between my fingers. I touched the trees. They were dusty and dry, but I knew it was time for the rains soon, then everything would blossom. I sucked the air into my lungs. It held the scents of my childhood memories, all those years when I lived outside and these desert plants and this red sand were my home. Oh, God, this was *my* place. I started to cry with the joy of being back home. I sat down under a tree and felt at the same time overwhelming happiness that I was back where I belonged, and deep sadness that I missed it so much. Looking around me, I wondered how I could have stayed away so long. It was like opening a door that I hadn't dared open before today, and finding a part of me that I'd forgotten. When I walked back to the village, everyone gathered around me, shaking my hand. "Welcome, sister."

Then we found out that nothing was what we expected. The woman who'd claimed to be my mother was not, and nobody knew how to find my family. The guys from the BBC were despondent; they didn't have the money in their budget to come back a second time. Gerry kept saying, "Oh, no, without this portion, there's no ending. And without this ending, there's no real story to the whole film. It's all wasted. What are we going to do?"

We combed the village, asking everybody if they'd heard of my family, or had any information about them. People were all anxious to help, and word of our mission spread quickly. Later that day, an older man walked up to me and said, "Do you remember me?"

"No."

"Well, I'm Ismail; I'm the same tribe as your father. I'm a very close friend of his." And then I realized who he was and felt ashamed for not recognizing him, but I hadn't seen him since I was a little girl. "I think I know where your family is. I think I can find your mother, but I'll need money for gas." Right away, I thought, *Oh, no. How can I trust this guy? Are all these people trying to con us? If I give this guy some money, he's just going to bugger off and we'll probably never see him again.* He went on, "I have this truck here, but it's not much. . . ."

Ismail pointed to a pickup truck—the type you'd never see anyplace but Africa or a junkyard in America. On the passenger's side the windshield was shattered; on the driver's side it was missing altogether. This meant that all the sand and flies in the desert would come sailing into his face as he drove. The wheels were warped and dented from driving over rocks. The body looked like someone had taken a sledgehammer to it. I shook my head. "Hold on a minute, let me talk to the guys."

I went to find Gerry and said, "This man over here thinks he knows where my family is. But he says he needs some money for gas to go look for them."

"Well, how are we going to trust him?"

"You're right, but we have to take a chance. We have no choice." They agreed and gave him some cash. The man hopped in his truck and took off immediately, raising a cloud of dust. I saw Gerry staring after him with a depressed look on his face, as if to say, "There went more money wasted."

I patted him on the back and said, "Don't worry. We're going to find my mother—I promise you. By the third day." My prophecy did little to ease the crew's minds. We had eight days here before the plane would come back to pick us up. And that was it. We couldn't say to the pilots, "Uh, yeah, we're not quite ready, try us again next week." Our tickets were scheduled for return from Addis Ababa to London; we would have to leave, and that would be the end of it, Mama or no Mama.

I had a good time hanging out with the villagers in their huts, sharing their food, but the English guys did not fare so well. They found a building with busted-out windows to sleep in, and rolled out their sleeping bags. They had brought some books and a flashlight, but they couldn't sleep at night because the mosquitoes drove them crazy. The BBC crew was living on canned beans, and complaining they were sick of their food, and there was nothing else to eat.

One afternoon, a Somali man decided he'd give them a treat and brought around a beautiful little baby goat; the guys were all petting it. Later, he brought it back skinned, and proudly presented it: "Here's your dinner." The guys looked shocked, but didn't say anything. I borrowed a pot and built a fire, then cooked the goat with some rice. When the Somali man left, they said, "You don't think we're going to eat that, do you?"

"Yes, of course. Why not?"

"Oh, forget it, Waris."

"Well, why didn't you say something?" They explained they

felt it would be rude, because the man was trying to be polite, but after petting the little goat, they couldn't eat it. They never touched it again.

My three-day deadline for finding Mama passed with no sign of her. Gerry grew more anxious by the day. I tried to reassure these guys that my mother was coming, but they thought I was being ludicrous. I said, "Look. I promise you my mother will be here tomorrow evening by six o'clock." I don't know why I had this belief, but it just came to me, so I told them.

Gerry and the guys started ribbing me about my latest prediction. "What? Yeah? How do you know that? Oh, yes, Waris knows! She predicts everything. She knows! Just like she predicts the rain!" They were laughing because I kept telling them when it was going to rain, because I could smell it.

"Well, it did rain, didn't it?" I demanded.

"Oh, come on, Waris. You were just lucky."

"It has nothing to do with luck. I'm back in my element now—I know this place. We survived here on our instincts, my friends." They started looking sideways at each other. "Okay. Don't believe me. You'll see—six o'clock."

The next day I was sitting talking to an elderly lady when Gerry jogged up at about ten minutes to six. "You're not going to believe it!"

"What?"

"Your mother—I think your mother is here." I stood up and smiled. "But, we're not sure. The man is back and he's got a woman with him; he says it's your mom. Come have a look."

The news had spread like a brushfire through the village; our little drama had definitely been the biggest thing to happen here for God knows how long. Everyone wanted to find out: Is this Waris's mother or just another impostor? By now it was nearly dark and a crowd gathered around us till I could barely walk. Gerry led me down a little alleyway. Up ahead was the man's pickup truck with the hole in the windshield, and a woman was climbing down from the seat. I couldn't see her face, but from the way she wore her scarf I could tell immediately that it was my mother. I ran to her and grabbed her. "Oh, Mama!"

She said, "I drive for miles and miles with this awful truck—and oh, Allah, what a horrible ride that was! And we're driving two solid days and nights—all for this?"

I turned to Gerry and laughed. "It's her!"

I told Gerry that they had to leave us alone for the next couple of days, and he kindly agreed. Talking to Mama was awkward; my Somali, I discovered, was pathetic. Tougher than that was the fact that we'd become strangers. At first, we just discussed little everyday things. But the gladness I felt at seeing her overcame the gap between us; I enjoyed just sitting close to her. Mama and Ismail had driven for two days and two nights straight, and I could see she was exhausted. She had aged a great deal in fifteen years—the result of a relentlessly hard life in the desert.

Papa wasn't with her. He was off searching for water when the truck came. My mother said Papa was getting old, too. He would go off chasing the clouds looking for rain, but he desperately needed glasses because his eyesight was terrible. When Mama left, he'd been gone for eight days, and she hoped he hadn't gotten lost. I thought back to how I remembered Papa, and realized how much he'd obviously changed. When I left home, he'd been able to find us even if the family moved on without him, and even on the blackest night with no moon.

My little brother, Ali, was also with her, along with one of my cousins, who happened to be visiting my mother when Ismail came. Ali wasn't my little brother anymore, however. At six four he towered over me, which pleased him no end. I kept holding Ali, and he would cry, "Get off now! I'm not a baby no more. I'm getting married."

"Married! How old are you?"

"I don't know. Old enough to get married."

"Well, I don't care. You're still my baby brother. Come here—" And I'd grab him and rub his head. My cousin laughed at this. I said to him, "I used to whip your ass!"—I used to baby-sit him when he was little and his family came to visit us.

"Yeah? Well, come try it now." He started shoving me and dancing around.

"Oh, no, don't!" I cried. "Don't even try. I'll beat you up." My cousin was getting married soon, too. "If you want to make it to your wedding day, boy, don't mess with me."

At night, Mama slept in the hut of one of the families there in Galadi who had taken us in. I slept outside with Ali—just like in the old days. As we lay there at night, I felt such a state of peace and happiness. We'd stare at the stars and talk deep into the night: "Remember the time we tied up Papa's little wife?'—and then both of us would roar.

Ali was so shy at first, but he confided, "You know, I really miss you. You've been gone for so long. It's so strange to think you're a woman now and I'm a man." It felt wonderful to be back with my family again, and talk and laugh and argue in my language about familiar things.

All the villagers were incredibly generous to us. We had invitations to a different home each day for lunch and dinner. Everybody wanted to spoil us and show us off, and hear all the stories about where we'd been. "Oh, come on, you've got to meet my child, meet my granny"—and they'd drag us off and introduce us. And none of this was about my being a "supermodel," because they had no idea about any of that. I was one of them—a nomad—and I'd come back home.

My mother, bless her heart, couldn't understand what I did for a living, no matter how hard I tried to explain. "Now, what is it again? What's modeling? You do what? What does that mean exactly?" At some point, someone traveling through the desert brought my mother a copy of *The Sunday Times* of London with my picture on the cover. Somali people are fiercely proud, and they were delighted to see a Somali woman on the cover of this English newspaper. Mama looked at it and said, "It's Waris! Oh, my daughter!" She carried it around showing all the villagers.

She got over her shyness after that first night, and quickly warmed up enough to boss me around: "You don't cook like *that*, Waris! Tsk-tsk, come, now! Let me show you. Don't you cook in that place where you live?"

Next, my brother started asking me what I thought about this and that. I'd tease him, "Oh—please shut up, Ali. You're just stupid, ignorant bush people. You've lived here too long and you don't know what you're talking about."

"Oh, yeah? You're famous, so you come home and put on your bullshit Western attitude? Now you live in the West and you know everything?"

We argued back and forth for hours. I didn't want to hurt their feelings, but I figured if I didn't tell them certain things, who else was going to? "Well, I don't know everything, but I've seen a lot and learned a lot I didn't know living back in the bush. And it's not all about cows and camels. I can tell you other things."

"Like what?"

"Well, for one thing you're destroying your environment by cutting all the trees. You cut all the little trees before they have a chance to grow, using the saplings to make pens for these stupid animals." I pointed at a nearby goat. "It's not right."

"What do you mean?"

"Well, the whole land is a desert now because we've cut all the trees."

"The land is a desert because it doesn't rain, Waris! It rains in the north and they've got trees."

"That's why it rains there! It rains *because* there's a forest there. And every other day you're cutting any little twig, so no forest ever has a chance to grow here." They didn't know whether to believe this bizarre idea or not, but there was one topic they felt confident I couldn't argue with.

My mother started. "Why are you not married?" This subject was still an open wound with me after all these years. As far as I was concerned it was the issue that had cost me my home and family. I know my father had meant well, but he'd offered me a terrible choice: do what he said, and ruin my life by marrying that old man, or run away, and give up everything I knew and loved. The price I paid for my freedom was enormous, and I hoped I'd never have to force a child of mine to make such a painful decision.

"Mama, why must I marry? Do I *have* to be married? Don't you want to see me a success—strong, independent? I mean, if I'm not married, it's just because I haven't found the right man yet. When I find him, *then* it will be time."

"Well, I want grandchildren."

Now they decided to all gang up on me. My cousin joined in: "Too old now. Who'd want to marry you? Too old." He shook his head at the horror of anybody marrying a twenty-eight-year-old woman.

I threw my hands up. "And who wants to get married if you're going to force them to? Why are you two getting married?" I pointed at Ali and my cousin. "I bet somebody pushed you into it."

"No, no." They both agreed.

"Well, okay, but just because you're boys. But as a girl, I have no say. I'm supposed to marry who you tell me to, when you tell me to. What is that shit? Who came up with that idea?"

"Oh, shut up, Waris," my brother groaned.

"You shut up, too!"

When we had two days left, Gerry said we had to start filming. He got several scenes of me with my mother. But Mama had never seen a camera before and she hated it. She said, "Get that thing out of my face. I don't want that," and she'd swat at the cameraman. "Waris—tell him to get that thing out of my face." I told her it was okay. "Is he looking at me? Or is he looking at you?"

"He's looking at both of us."

"Well, tell him I don't want to look at *him*. He's not going to hear what I say, is he?" I tried to explain the process to her, but I knew it was hopeless.

"Yeah, Mama. He hears everything you say," I said with a laugh. The cameraman kept asking me what we were laughing about. "Just the absurdity of it all . . ." I answered.

The crew spent another day filming me, as I walked through the desert alone. I saw a little boy watering his camel at a well, and I asked him if I could feed it. I held a bucket up to the animal's mouth for the crew. Throughout all this, it was hard for me to hold back my tears.

The day before we left, one of the women in the village did my fingernails with henna. I held my hand up to the camera, and it looked like I had mushy cow poop globbed on the tip of each finger. But I felt like a queen. These were the ancient beauty rituals of my people—the type they normally save for a bride. That night we had a celebration and the villagers were all dancing, clapping, and singing. It was like old times I remembered from childhood, when everyone would rejoice over the rain—such an uninhibited feeling of freedom and joy.

The next morning before the plane came to get us, I got up early and had breakfast with my mother. I asked her if she would like to come back and live with me in England or the States.

"But what would I do?" she said.

"That's precisely it. I don't want you to do anything. You've done enough work in your time. It's time for you to rest—put your feet up. I want to spoil you."

"No. I can't do that. First of all, your father's getting old. He needs me. I need to be with him. And second, I have to take care of the children."

"What do you mean, children? All of us are grown!"

"Well, your father's children. Remember what's-her-name, that little girl he married?"

"Y-e-s-s."

"Well, she had five kids. But she couldn't take it anymore. I guess our life was too tough for her, or she couldn't handle your father. Anyway, she ran away—disappeared."

"Mama . . . how dare you. You're getting too old for that kind of stuff! You shouldn't be working that hard—chasing kids around at your age."

"Well, your father's getting old, too, and he needs me. Besides, I can't just sit around. If I sit down, I'm going to be old. I can't stay still after all these years—that would drive me crazy. I have to keep moving. No. If you want to do something for me, get me a place in Africa, in Somalia, that I can go to when I'm tired. This is my home. This is all I've ever known."

I gave her a big hug. "I love you, Mama, and I'm coming back for you, don't you forget that. I'm coming back for you . . ."

She smiled and waved good-bye.

Once we got aboard the plane, I broke down. I didn't know when or if I'd ever see my mother again. While I was staring out the window crying, watching the village, then the desert, slip away, the crew was filming a close-up shot of me.

16.

THE BIG APPLE

In the spring of 1995, I finished the documentary with the BBC, which they titled *A Nomad in New York*. And I was indeed a nomad after all these years, since I still didn't have a real home. I moved around, following the work: New York, London, Paris, Milan. I'd stay with friends, or in hotels. What few things I owned—a few photos, some books and CDs—were stashed away at Nigel's house in Wales. Since most of my work was in New York, I spent more time there than anywhere. At one point I actually rented my first apartment—a studio in SoHo. Later, I had a place in the Village, then a house on West Broadway. But I didn't like any of these places. The place on Broadway was total madness—it drove me crazy. Every time a car passed by, it sounded like it was inside my house. There was a firehouse on the corner, and I heard sirens going off all night. I couldn't get enough rest, and after ten months I gave up and went back to my nomadic existence.

That fall I did the runway shows in Paris, then decided to skip the shows in London and come straight to New York. I felt it was time to get my own place and settle down a bit, and while I was apartment hunting, I stayed in the Village with one of my closest friends, George. While I was there one night, another friend of George's, Lucy, had a birthday. She wanted to go out on the town to celebrate, but George announced he was too tired, and he had to get up early in the morning for work. I volunteered to go out with Lucy.

We walked out of the house, with no idea of where we were going. On Eighth Avenue, I stopped and pointed out my old apartment. "I used to live up there, above that jazz place. They always played good music, but I never went in." As we stood there, I listened to the music coming out the door. "Hey, come on, let's go in. You want to?"

"Nah. I want to go to Nell's."

"Oh, come on. Let's go in and just check it out. I really like this music they're playing—I feel like dancing."

Reluctantly, Lucy agreed to go in. I walked down the steps into a tiny little club, and straight ahead was the band. I walked up to the stage and stopped. The first person I saw was the drummer; the light was shining on him in the otherwise dark room. He was banging away, and I just stood there staring at him. He had kind of a big seventies Afro, with a funky style. When Lucy caught up to me, I turned to her: "No, no, no. We're staying. Sit down, have a drink. We're staying for a little bit." The band was really jamming and I started dancing like crazy. Lucy joined in, and soon all the other people, who had been kind of subdued, sitting around just watching, got up and started dancing with us.

Hot and thirsty, I got a drink and stood next to a woman in the audience. I said, "Oh, this is bright music. Who are they, anyway?"

She said, "I don't know because they're all freelancers, but my husband is the one playing sax."

"Uh-huh. And who's the one playing drums?"

She smiled slowly. "Sorry, but I don't know." In a few

minutes the band took a break, and when the drummer walked by, this lady grabbed his arm and said, "Excuse me, but my friend would like to meet you."

"Oh, yeah? Who's that?"

"Her"—and with that she pushed me forward. I was so embarrassed I didn't know what to say.

Finally, after standing there frozen for a few moments, I said, "Hi." *Play it cool, Waris.* "I like the music."

"Thanks."

"What's your name?"

"Dana," he said, and looked around shyly.

"Oh." And he just turned and walked away. Damn! But I wasn't letting him get away that easily. I followed him to where he sat down with his buddies from the band, yanked up a chair, and sat next to him. When the drummer turned around and saw me, he jumped. I scolded, "Wasn't I just talking to you? That was rude. You walked away from me, you know?" Dana looked at me, bewildered, then cracked up laughing and doubled over the table.

"What is your name?" he said, when he straightened himself up.

"It doesn't matter now, anyway," I replied in my cockiest manner, sticking my nose in the air. But then we began to talk about all kinds of things until he said he had to play again.

"Are you leaving? Who are you here with?" he asked.

"My friend. She's in the crowd over there." On his next break, he said the band only had a couple of more sets, and if I wanted to, after they finished we could go somewhere. When he came back, we sat talking and talking about anything and everything. Finally, I said, "It's too smoky in here. I can't breathe. You want to go outside?"

"Okay. We can go outside and sit on the steps." When we reached the top of the stairs he stopped. "Can I ask you something? Can I have a hug?"

I looked at him like it was the most natural request in the

world, like I'd known him forever. So I hugged him really tight, and I knew that was it, just like I knew about going to London, and I knew about modeling. I knew this shy drummer with the funky Afro was my man. It was too late to go anyplace that night, but I told him to call me the next day and gave him George's number. "I have appointments in the morning. But call me *exactly* at three o'clock. Okay?" I just wanted to see if he would call me when I told him to.

Later, he told me that on the way home that night, he went to catch the subway to his place uptown in Harlem. When he was entering the station, he looked up and there was a huge billboard of my face staring down at him. He'd never noticed it before, and had no idea I was a model.

The next day the phone rang at twenty past three. I jerked up the receiver. "YOU'RE LATE."

"I'm sorry. Do you want to meet me for dinner?" We met at a little café in the Village and again talked and talked. Now that I know him, I realize how unlike him that was, because he's phenomenally quiet with anyone he doesn't know. Finally I started laughing. Dana looked startled. "What are you laughing about?"

"You're going to think I'm crazy."

"Go ahead. I already think you're crazy."

"I'm going to have your baby." He did not look pleased to find out he would be the future father of my child. Instead, he stared at me with a look that said, *This woman is really crazy, not just hey, let's party, crazy.* "I know you think that's strange, but I just wanted to tell you. But anyway, drop it. Let's forget it."

He sat silently staring at me; I could see he was shocked. And no wonder. I didn't even know his last name. Later, he said he was thinking, *I don't want to see her again. I've got to get rid of this woman. She's like that loony stalker in* Fatal Attraction.

Dana walked me home after dinner, but he was very quiet. The next day I was thoroughly disgusted with myself. I couldn't believe I'd said something so obviously uncool. But at the time, it just seemed like the most normal thing to say, like "Oh, it's going to rain today." Not surprisingly, I didn't hear from him for a week. Finally, I gave in and called him. "Where are you?" he asked.

"At my friend's. You want to get together?"

"Oh, God. Yes, all right. We can go for lunch."

"I love you."

"I love you, too." I put the phone down in absolute shock and horror that I'd just told this man I loved him after I swore to myself I'd be good. No more talk about babies—any of that— and now here I go and tell him I love him. *Oh, Waris, what is wrong with you?* Always, when any man was interested in me, I ran. I would disappear. Now here I was, chasing this man I barely knew. The night I met Dana, I was wearing a green sweater and had my hair in a wild Afro. He later told me that everywhere he turned that night, all he could see was GREEN SWEATER WITH AFRO. I explained that if I wanted something I went after it, and for some reason—for the first time in my life—I very much wanted a man. The thing I couldn't explain was why I felt like I'd known him all my life.

Dana and I met for lunch and again talked and talked and talked about everything in the world. Two weeks later I was living with him at his place in Harlem. After six months we decided we wanted to get married.

After we'd been together nearly a year, one day Dana said unexpectedly, "I think you're pregnant."

I cried, "What are you talking about, for God's sake!"

"Come on, we're going to the pharmacy." I protested, but he was not giving in. We went to the pharmacy and bought a home pregnancy test. It turned out positive.

"You don't believe this piece of shit, do you?" I asked, pointing at the box.

He picked up the pack and pulled out another one. "Do it

again." That one was positive as well. I had been feeling sick, but I always felt sick when it was time for my period. But this time was different. I felt worse than usual, with even more pain. However, I didn't think I was pregnant. I thought something critical was wrong with me—I thought I was going to die. I went to the doctor and explained the situation. He did a blood test and I waited an agonizing three days to hear from him. *Hell! What is going on here? I've got some horrible disease and he just doesn't want to have to tell me?*

Finally, I came home one afternoon and Dana said, "Uh, yeah, the doctor called."

My hand flew to my throat. "Oh, God, what did he say?"

"He said he'd talk to you."

"Didn't you ask him any questions!?"

"Look, he said he'd call you tomorrow around eleven or twelve."

That was the longest night of my life, lying there wondering what my future would hold. The next day when the phone rang, I grabbed it. The doctor said, "I have news for you. You're not alone." *There you go—that's it! Not alone—full of tumors all over my body!*

"Oh, no. What does that mean?"

"You're pregnant. You're two months pregnant." And when I heard those words I just flew over the moon. Dana was delighted, too, because all his life he'd wanted to be a father. We both knew instantly the baby was going to be a boy. But my first concern was about the baby's health. I went to an obstetrician the second we found out I was expecting. When the doctor did the ultrasound, I told her not to tell me the sex.

"Please, just tell me, is the baby okay?"

She said, "It's a fine baby, perfectly fine." Those were the words I was waiting to hear.

Of course, there was one very large barrier to my happy marriage to Dana: Nigel. When I was four months pregnant, we decided to go to Wales together and deal with him once and for all. By the time we arrived in London, I was ill with morning sickness and a bad cold. We stayed at a friend's house, and after I recuperated a couple of days, I got up the nerve to call Nigel. But when I called him he said he had a cold, too, so I'd have to postpone my visit.

Dana and I waited in London for over a week before Nigel was feeling up to a visit. I called and gave him the train schedule so he could pick us up at the station, and said, "I just want to let you know that Dana is coming with me. And I don't want any problems, okay?"

"I don't want to see him. I'll tell you that now. This is between me and you."

"Nigel—"

"I don't care. I don't care. This has nothing to do with him."

"It has a lot to do with him now. He's my fiancé. He's the man I'm going to marry. Okay? And whatever I have to do here, he's doing it with me."

"I don't want to see him and that's it." So Nigel had it in his head that I was taking the train to Wales alone. When I got off, he was waiting, leaning up against a post in the parking lot, smoking a cigarette as usual. He looked worse than the last time I'd seen him. His hair was longer now, and he had dark circles under his eyes.

I turned to Dana and said, "Okay, there he is. Now be cool."

We walked over to him, and before I could get a word out of my mouth, Nigel said, "I told you I didn't want to see him. I told you that. It was very clear. I made it very clear. I want to see you alone."

Dana dropped the bags on the pavement. "Look, you don't talk to her like that, and you don't talk to me like that. Why do you want to see her alone? What is the deal here? You want to see her alone? Well, I don't want you to see her alone. And if you say it one more time, I'm going to kick your fucking ass!"

Nigel turned even paler than he already was. "Well . . . there's not enough room in the car."

"I don't give a fuck about your car. We can take a cab. Let's just get this thing over with."

By now Nigel was moving rapidly toward his car, calling over his shoulder, "No, no, no. That's not how I do things." He jumped in, started the engine, and roared past us as Dana and I stood there next to our bags, watching him drive by. We decided it was best to find a hotel. Luckily, there was a bed-and-breakfast right by the station. It was a depressing little dump, but under the circumstances, that was the least of our worries. We went out and ordered Indian food, but had no appetite, so we basically just sat there staring at it glumly, until we decided to go back to our room.

The next morning I called Nigel again. "I just want to get my things. Okay? If you don't want to deal with this, then forget it. Just give me my stuff." No deal. Now Dana and I had to move to a hotel because the bed-and-breakfast, where we had spent the night, was booked solid, and it looked like we better get comfortable. With Nigel, only God knew how long this process would take. We found another place to stay, and after we'd moved, I called again. "Look, why are you being such an asshole? Why are you doing this? How many years has this been going on? Seven? Eight? Now, come on."

"Okay. You want to see me, all right. But just you. I'll pick you up from the hotel, but if he comes out, that's it. I'll drive away. No, just you." I sighed, but couldn't see any other way out of this mess so I agreed.

I hung up the phone and explained the situation to Dana. "Please, Dana, just let me go over there alone and see if I can talk to him. Just do this for me."

"All right, if you think it's going to work. But if he touches you, he's had it. I'm telling you now, I don't like this shit, but if that's what you want to do, I can't stop you." I told Dana to stay around the hotel and I'd call him if I needed him.

Nigel picked me up and we drove to the cottage he was renting. We went inside and he made me a cup of tea. I said,

"Look, Nigel. This is the man I'm going to marry, and I'm pregnant with his child. There's going to be no more bullshit of your little fantasy world where I'm your precious wife and we have a life together. It's over. Okay? Got it? Now, come on, let's just get on with it. I want a divorce now, this week. And I'm not going back to New York until we get this garbage straightened out."

"Well, first of all, I'm not divorcing you unless you give me all the money you owe me."

"Um, I owe *you* money? How much? Who's been working and giving you money for years now?"

"That all went to pay for the food you were eating."

"Oh, I see. When I wasn't even here. Well, since you're so obsessed with this money, how much is it?"

"At least forty thousand pounds."

"Hah!! Where am I going to get that kind of money? I haven't got it."

"I don't care. I don't care. I don't care. I mean, this is how it is. You owe me money, and I'm not going anywhere, and I'm not giving you a divorce or anything else. You're never going to be free, unless you come up with the money you owe me. I sold my house because of you."

"You sold your house because you couldn't pay the mortgage, and I got sick of paying it. All you had to do was get yourself a job, but you couldn't even do that."

"What? Job to do what? What kind of job was I going to get—work at McDonald's?"

"If that's what you had to do to pay your mortgage, why not?"

"That's not what I do best."

"What the fuck did you ever do best?"

"I'm an environmentalist."

"Yeah, right. I got you a job and they sacked you and told you not to come back. You've got nobody but yourself to blame, and I'm not putting up with this shit. And I'm not giving you a fucking penny. You know what? You can take your stupid passport and shove it up your ass. There's obviously no point talking to you anymore. Ours was never a real marriage, and it wasn't legal, because we were never intimate."

"That's not true. Not now. That's not how the law reads now. You're married to me and I'll never let you go, Waris. Your baby is going to be a bastard for the rest of his life."

I sat there staring at him, and any pity I ever felt hardened into hatred. I realized the awful irony of the situation. I decided to marry him when he was so eager to help me "because it was Allah's will." Since his sister was a good friend of mine, I felt if there were any problems, she'd intercede. But she wasn't around. "I'm getting a divorce, Nigel, with or without your consent. We have nothing else to talk about."

He looked at me solemnly for a minute, then said quietly, "Well, if I don't have you, I have nothing. I'll kill you, then kill myself."

I froze, trying to decide my next move, then started bluffing. "Dana is coming here to get me. I wouldn't try anything if I were you." I knew I had to get out of there immediately, because this time he'd really gone over the edge. I bent over to pick up my bag from the floor, and he shoved me from behind. I went crashing into the stereo face first, then rolled off onto the hardwood floor, landing on my back. I just lay there, scared to move. Oh, my God—my baby! I was so paralyzed with fear that I'd harmed my baby. Slowly I got to my feet.

"Oh, fuck, are you all right?" he cried.

"Yeah. I'm okay," I said calmly. I realized now what a fool I'd been to come here alone, and just wanted to get out in one piece. "It's okay. I'm all right." He helped me up. Pretending to be very collected, I put my jacket on.

"I'll take you home. Get in the fucking car." Now he was angry again. While he was driving, I sat there thinking: *He hates this baby and nothing would make him happier than to see it dead. Maybe he's going to try to drive us off a cliff?* I put my seat belt on. In the meantime, he was screaming, cursing, calling me every name he could think of. I just sat there, quietly staring straight ahead, afraid to say a word or he'd hit me. By this point, I was so numb, I didn't even care about myself, but I cared deeply about my baby. I'm a fighter, and if I hadn't been pregnant, I would have ripped his balls off.

When we got to the hotel, he screamed, "That's it? You're just going to sit there and say nothing—after all I've done for you!" The second he stopped the car, he reached across me, opened the door, and pushed me out onto the ground. One of my legs was still inside, lying across the floorboard; I struggled to untangle myself from the car and ran inside and up to our room.

By the time Dana opened the door, tears were pouring down my face. "What happened? What did he do to you?"

I could see it all clearly: if I told Dana the truth, he'd kill Nigel, then he'd go to prison and I'd get to raise my baby alone. "Nothing. He's just being an asshole, as usual. Wouldn't give me my stuff." I blew my nose.

"That's it? Oh, Waris, forget that shit. That's not worth crying over." Dana and I took the first flight we could get back to New York.

Now, looking back on this time, despite the way he behaved towards me at the end, I feel grateful for the fact that he often went to battle on my behalf and helped me so much when I was really alone in Britain.

When I was eight months pregnant, an African photographer heard I was having a baby and said he wanted to photograph me. He asked me to come to Spain where he was working. By this point I felt great, so I wasn't afraid to travel. I knew I wasn't supposed to fly after six months, but I wore a loose sweater and sneaked on board the flight. He did some brilliant shots for *Marie Claire*.

But I had to fly pregnant one more time. Twenty days before I gave birth, I flew to Nebraska to be with Dana's family so they could help me with the baby after he was born. I stayed with Dana's parents in Omaha. He had gigs scheduled playing in the clubs, and planned to fly out the following week. Shortly after I arrived, I got up one morning and noted my stomach felt funny; I kept wondering what I'd eaten the night before that would cause such indigestion. This continued for that day, but I didn't mention it. By the next morning I had a really bad stomachache. Then it occurred to me that maybe this wasn't a stomachache. Maybe I was having the baby.

I called Dana's mom at work and said, "Look, I've got this weird pain and it comes and goes. It was happening all day yesterday and last night. But it's getting worse. I don't know what I could have eaten, but it feels strange."

"Waris, for God's sake. You're having contractions!"

Oh! Then I was really happy, because I was so ready to have the baby. I called Dana in New York and told him, "I think I'm having the baby!"

"No, no, no! You can't have it till I get there. HOLD THAT BABY! I'm coming, I'm getting on a plane."

"You fucking come and hold it! How am I supposed to do that? Hold the baby!" God, silly men! But I did want Dana to be there for the delivery of our first baby, and I was going to be disappointed if he didn't see it. After I had talked to his mother earlier, she called the hospital, and the nurse called to check on me. She said if I wanted to have the baby, I should walk around. I figured if I *didn't* want to have the baby, that meant I should do the reverse, so I lay absolutely still.

Dana didn't arrive until the following evening. By this time I'd been having contractions for three days. When his father went to pick him up at the airport, I was panting hard. "Oh, oh, oh, EEE! AH! SHIT! OH GOD!"

"Count, Waris, count!" Dana's mom yelled. We decided it was time to go to the hospital, but we couldn't go because

Dana's father had the car. When he drove up, they didn't even make it into the house before we started yelling, "Get back to the car, we're going to the hospital!"

We arrived at the hospital at ten o'clock; at ten o'clock the next morning, I was still in labor. "I want to swing upside down from the tree!" I kept screaming. This I knew was pure animal instinct, like a monkey's instinct, because that's how animals do it. They move around, they sit, they squat, they run and swing until they give birth. They don't just lie there. And since that day, Dana still calls me Monkey. In a falsetto voice he'll cry, "Ahhh, I want to swing upside down from the tree!"

While we were in the delivery room, the expectant father would coach, "Breathe, baby, just breathe."

"FUCK! Get the fuck away from me. I'll fucking kill you, you motherfucker!" Oh, my God, I wanted to shoot him. I wanted to die, and before I died, I wanted to make sure I killed him.

Finally, at noon, the moment came. I was so grateful to that doctor in London who operated on me, because I couldn't even imagine trying to go through that delivery when I was still sewn up. And then, after waiting nine months and suffering for three days, magically there he was. Ooooh! After all this time, I was so glad to see him—this little, little thing. He was so beautiful, with silky black hair, a tiny, tiny mouth, and the longest of feet and fingers. He stretched over twenty inches but weighed only six pounds and thirteen ounces. Immediately my son said, "Ah," and began looking around the room, very curious. *This is what it's all about, then? This is it? This is the light?* Must have felt good after being in the dark for nine months.

I had told the staff that as soon as the baby was born, I wanted them to lay him on my chest, with all that goo and everything. They did, and in that instant I first held him, I realized that the old cliché that every mother told me was true: When you hold that baby, suddenly you forget the pain. In that moment, there is no pain. There is only joy.

I named the baby Aleeke, which in Somali means strong lion. But right now, with his tiny bow mouth, chubby cheeks, and halo of curls, he looks more like a little black Cupid than a lion. His big, smooth forehead looks exactly like mine. When I talk to him, he puckers his mouth like a tweety bird preparing to sing. Since the moment he was born, he's been eternally curious, quietly looking at everything and exploring his new world.

When I was a little girl, I so much looked forward to coming home at night after tending my animals, and lying in Mama's lap. She would stroke my head, giving me such a feeling of peace and security. Now I do this to Aleeke, and just as I did, he loves it too. I'll massage his head and he immediately falls asleep in my arms.

From the day he was born, my life changed. The happiness I get from him is everything to me now. I pushed aside all the stupid little things that I used to complain and worry about. I realized that none of that matters at all. Life—the gift of life— is what matters, and that's what giving birth to my son made me remember.

17.

THE AMBASSADOR

In my culture, a woman earns a badge of respect when she becomes a mother. She has brought another human being into this world, contributed to the gift of life. When Aleeke was born, I, too, was a mama, a woman who had come of age. After going through the cycle of womanhood that began prematurely with my circumcision at age five, and came full circle with my baby's birth when I was about thirty, I had even more respect for my own mother. I understood what incredible strength the women in Somalia possess to bear the burden they carry simply because they're born female. As a woman living in the West, I struggled to do what I had to do, and some days didn't think I'd make it: trying to work scrubbing floors at McDonald's when my periods were so painful I thought I'd pass out. Having surgery to open the crude scars of my genitals so that I could urinate properly. Waddling around nine months pregnant, taking the subway uptown to Harlem, climbing the stairs, and shopping for food at the market. Spending three days in labor and thinking I

---

would surely die right there in the delivery room in front of the doctors.

The reality is that I'm the lucky one. What about the girl back in the bush, walking miles and miles to water her goats, while she's in such pain from her period that she can barely stand up straight? Or the wife who will be sewn back up with a needle and thread like a piece of cloth as soon as she gives birth, so her vagina will remain tight for her husband? Or the woman nine months pregnant hunting for food in the desert to feed her other eleven starving children? Or what happens to the new wife who's still sewn up tight, and it's time for her first baby to be born? What happens when she goes out into the desert alone, as my mother did, and tries to deliver it by herself? Unfortunately, I know the answer to that question. Many bleed to death out there alone, and if they're lucky, their husbands will find them before the vultures and hyenas do.

As I grew older and more educated, I learned that I was not alone. The health problems I've coped with since my circumcision also plague millions of girls and women throughout the world. Because of a ritual of ignorance, most of the women on the continent of Africa live their lives in pain. Who is going to help the woman in the desert—like my mother—with no money and no power? Somebody must speak out for the little girl with no voice. And since I began as a nomad just like them, I felt it was my destiny to help them.

I could never explain why so many things happened in my life by pure chance. But I don't really believe in the concept of pure chance; there has to be more to our lives than that. God saved me from a lion in the desert when I ran away from home, and from that moment on, I felt he had a plan for me, some reason to keep me alive. But if it was for a reason, what was that reason?

Some time back, a writer for the fashion magazine *Marie Claire* made an appointment to interview me. Before our meeting, I gave a lot of thought to what I wanted to say in the article. When I met the writer, Laura Ziv, for lunch, I took one look at her face and liked her right away. I said, "You know, I don't know what kind of story you wanted from me—but all of that fashion model stuff's been done a million times. If you promise to publish it, I'll give you a real story."

She said, "Oh? Well, I'll do my best," and switched on her tape recorder. I began telling her the story of my circumcision when I was a child. Suddenly, halfway through the interview, she started crying and turned off the tape.

"Oh, what's the matter with you?"

"I mean, it's horrible . . . it's disgusting. I never dreamed such things still happen today."

"Now there you go. That's the whole point, people in the West don't know. Do you think you can put that in your magazine—your fabulously glossy, gorgeous magazine, which nobody reads but women?"

"I promise I'll do the best I can. But the decision will be up to my boss."

The next day after the interview, I felt stunned and embarrassed at what I'd done. Everybody would know my business now. My most personal secret. Even my closest friends didn't know what had happened to me as a little girl. Being from a very private culture in Somalia, it simply wasn't the type of thing I could ever talk about. Now here I was talking about it to millions of strangers. But finally I decided: Let it be. Lose your dignity if that's what it takes. So I did. I removed my dignity, as if I were taking off my clothes. I put it to the side and walked around without it. But I was also worried about the response of other Somalis; I could imagine them saying, "How dare you criticize our ancient traditions!" I could imagine them echoing my family when I saw them in Ethiopia: "You think because you moved to the West, you know everything?"

After much thought, I realized I needed to talk about my

circumcision for two reasons. First of all, it's something that bothers me deeply. Besides the health problems that I still struggle with, I will never know the pleasures of sex that have been denied me. I feel incomplete, crippled, and knowing that there's nothing I can do to change that is the most hopeless feeling of all. When I met Dana, I finally fell in love and wanted to experience the joys of sex with a man. But if you ask me today, "Do you enjoy sex?" I would say not in the traditional way. I simply enjoy being physically close to Dana because I love him.

All my life I've tried to think of a reason for my circumcision. Maybe if I could have thought of a good reason, I could accept what they'd done to me. But I could think of none. The longer I tried to think of a reason without finding one, the angrier I became. I needed to talk about my secret, because I kept it bottled up inside me all my life. Since I didn't have any family around me, no mother or sisters, there was no one I could share my grief with. I hate the term "victim" because it sounds so helpless. But when the gypsy woman butchered me, that's exactly what I was. However, as a grown woman, I was no longer a victim, and I could take action. By doing the *Marie Claire* article, I wanted the people who promote this torture to hear what it feels like from at least one woman, because all the females in my country are silenced.

It occurred to me that after people learned my secret, they were going to look at me oddly when they saw me on the street. I decided I didn't care. Because the second reason for doing the article was the hope of making people aware that this practice still occurs today. I've got to do it not only for me but for all the little girls in the world who are going through it now. Not hundreds, not thousands, but millions of girls are living with it and dying from it. It's too late to change my own circumstances, the damage has already been done; but maybe I can help save somebody else.

When my interview "The Tragedy of Female Circumcision" came out, the response was dramatic. Laura did a great job, and publishing it was a courageous act on the part of *Marie Claire*. The magazine and Equality Now, an organization that fights for women's rights, were swamped with letters of support. Like Laura the day I told her, the readers were obviously horrified:

> One month ago today I read with horror the story in the March issue of *Marie Claire* on female "circumcision," and have not been able to get it off my mind. I would find it difficult to believe that *anyone*, male or female, could forget or pass off something as cold and inhuman as this treatment of the gender which God created as man's friend and companion, his "helpmate." The Bible says men are to "love their wives." Even if living in a culture where God is not known to exist, people cannot help but realize that by the pain, trauma, and even death this inflicts on their women that it is SO WRONG! How can they continue to allow this to happen to their wives, daughters, and sisters? Surely they must know they are destroying their women in so many ways!
>
> God help us, we have to DO SOMETHING. I wake up thinking about it, I go to bed thinking about it, and throughout the day I cry about it! Surely with World Vision or another such organization these people can be educated and taught how their marriages and intimacy could be so much better for the men as well as for the women, *as it was meant to be*, and that women were born with certain body parts for good reason, just as men were!

And another:

> I just finished reading your article on Waris Dirie, and am sick to my soul that such torture and mutilation is still endured by little girls. I can hardly believe that something

this sadistic is being practiced today. The problems these women face their whole lives resulting from this are incredible. Tradition or not, these outrages against females worldwide need to end. Let me slice open one man's genitals and sew them back up and I can guarantee this practice would stop. How can you want to be with a woman physically when her pain is severe and never-ending? This story has brought me to tears and I am writing the Equality Now organization for information on how to help.

Another letter addressed to me read:

There are a lot of tragic stories that have been told, and there will be more told in the future, but Waris, there are not any more to be told of an entire culture that can be more horrifying than what these people are doing to their children. I cried and felt deeply when I read this. I want to do something to change things, but I don't know what one person can do.

I was relieved by the letters of support; I received only two negative responses criticizing me, and not surprisingly they came from Somalia.

I began giving more interviews and speaking at schools, community organizations, and basically anywhere I could to publicize the issue.

Then another stroke of fate occurred. A makeup artist was on board a plane flying from Europe to New York; she picked up *Marie Claire* and read my interview. During the flight she showed it to her employer, and said, "You should read this." Her employer happened to be Barbara Walters. Barbara later told me that she couldn't finish the article because it was so disturbing. However, it was a problem she felt needed to be addressed. She decided to do a segment for *20/20* using my story to make viewers aware of female circumcision. Ethel Bass Weintraub produced the award-winning segment titled "A Healing Journey."

While Barbara was interviewing me, I wanted to cry; I felt so naked. Telling the story in an article somehow put a distance between me and the reader. I only had to tell Laura, and we were just two women in a restaurant. But when they were filming me for 20/20, I knew the camera was doing a close-up of my face as I revealed secrets I had guarded my entire life; it was if someone had cut me open and exposed my soul.

"A Healing Journey" aired in the summer of 1997. Soon after that I received a call from my agency saying they had been contacted by the United Nations. The UN had seen the 20/20 segment and wanted me to contact them.

Events had taken another amazing turn. The United Nations Population Fund invited me to join their fight to stop female circumcision. Working with the World Health Organization, they had compiled some truly terrifying statistics that put the extent of the problem in perspective. After seeing those numbers, it became clear that this wasn't just my problem. Female circumcision, or as it is more aptly referred to today, female genital mutilation (FGM), occurs predominantly in twenty-eight countries in Africa. The UN estimates that this practice has been performed on 130 million girls and women. At least 2 million girls are at risk each year of being the next victims—that's 6,000 a day. The operations are usually performed in primitive circumstances by a midwife or village woman. They use no anesthetic. They'll cut the girl using whatever instruments they can lay their hands on: razor blades, knives, scissors, broken glass, sharp stones—and in some regions—their teeth. The process ranges in severity by geographic location and cultural practice. The most minimal damage is cutting away the hood of the clitoris, which will prohibit the girl from enjoying sex for the rest of her life. At the other end of the spectrum is infibulation, which is performed on 80 percent of the women in Somalia. This was the version I was subjected to. The aftermath of infibulation includes the immediate complications of shock, infection, damage to the urethra or anus, scar formation, tetanus, bladder infections, septicemia, HIV, and hepatitis B. Long-term complications include chronic and recurrent urinary and pelvic infections that can lead to sterility, cysts and abscesses around the vulva, painful neuromas, increasingly difficult urination, dysmenorrhea, the pooling of menstrual blood in the abdomen, frigidity, depression, and death.

When I imagine that this year two million more little girls will go through what I went through, it breaks my heart. It also makes me realize that each day this torture continues, angry women like myself will be produced, women who can never go back and recapture what was taken from them.

In fact, instead of dwindling, the number of girls being mutilated is growing. The large numbers of Africans who have emigrated to Europe and the United States have taken the practice with them. The federal Centers for Disease Control and Prevention estimates that 27,000 New York State women have had or *will* have the procedure performed. For this reason, many states are passing laws to make FGM illegal. Legislators feel that separate laws are necessary to protect the children at risk, because the families will claim it is their "religious right" to mutilate their daughters. Many times an African community will save enough money to bring a circumciser, like the gypsy woman, all the way from Africa to America. Then she'll cut a group of little girls all at once. When this is not possible, families take matters into their own hands. One father in New York City turned up the stereo so his neighbors couldn't hear the screams. Then he cut off his daughter's genitals with a steak knife.

With great pride, I accepted the UN's offer to become a Special Ambassador and join its fight. One of the highest honors of my position will be working with women like Dr. Nafis Sadik, the executive director of the UN's Population Fund. She is one of the first women who took up the fight against FGM, raising the issue at the International Conference on Population and Development in Cairo in 1994. I will travel back to Africa again soon to tell my story, and lend support to the UN.

For over four thousand years African cultures have mutilated their women. Many believe the Koran demands this, as the practice is nearly universal in Moslem countries. However, this is not the case; neither the Koran nor the Bible makes any mention of cutting women to please God. The practice is simply promoted and demanded by men—ignorant, selfish men—who want to assure their ownership of their woman's sexual favors. They demand their wives be circumcised. The mothers comply by circumcising their daughters, for fear their daughters will have no husbands. An uncircumcised woman is regarded as dirty, oversexed, and unmarriageable. In a nomadic culture like the one I was raised in, there is no place for an unmarried woman, so mothers feel it is their duty to make sure their daughters have the best possible opportunity— much as a Western family might feel it's their duty to send their daughter to good schools. There is no reason for the mutilation of millions of girls to occur every year except ignorance and superstition. And the legacy of pain, suffering, and death that results from it is more than enough reason for it to stop.

Working as a UN ambassador is the fulfillment of a dream so outrageous that I never dared dream it. Although I always felt I was different from my family and fellow nomads when I was growing up, I could have never foreseen a future for myself as an ambassador working for an organization that takes on solving the problems of the world. On an international level, the UN does what mothers do on a personal level: it gives comfort and provides security. I guess that's the only past inkling of my future role with the UN; during my early years my friends constantly referred to me as Mama. They teased me because I always wanted to mother them and look after everybody.

Many of those same friends have expressed concern that a religious fanatic will try to kill me when I go to Africa. After all, I'll be speaking out against a crime many fundamentalists consider a holy practice. I'm sure my work will be dangerous, and I admit to being scared; I'm especially worried now that I have a little boy to take care of. But my faith tells me to be strong, that God led me down this path for a reason. He has work for me to do. This is my mission. And I believe that long before the day I was born, God chose the day I will die, so I can't change that. In the meantime, I might as well take a chance, because that's what I've done all my life.

18.

THOUGHTS OF
HOME

Because I criticize the practice of female genital mutilation, some people think that I don't appreciate my culture. But they're so wrong. Oh, I thank God every day that I'm from Africa. Every day. I'm very proud to be Somali, and proud of my country. I guess some other cultures might consider that a very African way of thinking—you know, being proud for nothing. Arrogant, I guess you'd call it.

Other than the circumcision issue, I wouldn't trade with anyone the way I grew up. Living in New York, although everyone talks about family values, I've seen very little of them. I don't see families getting together like we did, singing, clapping, laughing. People here are disconnected from one another; there's no sense of belonging to a community.

Another benefit of growing up in Africa was that we were part of pure nature, pure life. I knew life—I wasn't sheltered from it. And it was real life—not some artificial substitute on television where I'm watching *other* people live life. From the beginning, I had the instinct for survival; I learned joy and pain at the same time. I learned that happiness is not what you have, because I never had anything, and I was so happy. The most treasured time in my life was back when my family and I were all together. I think of evenings when we'd sit around the fire after we'd eaten, and laugh about every little thing. And when the rains began and life was reborn, we celebrated.

When I was growing up in Somalia, we appreciated the simple things in life. We celebrated the rain because that meant we had water. Who in New York worries about water? Let it run from the tap while you walk away and do something else in the kitchen. It's always there when you need it. BOOM, you turn on the faucet and out it comes. It's when you don't have something that you appreciate it, and since we had nothing, we appreciated everything.

My family struggled every day to have enough food. Buying a sack of rice was a big occasion for us. In this country, however, the volume and variety of food is astonishing to anyone who comes here from a Third World nation. Yet, sadly, so many Americans are preoccupied with *not* eating. On one side of the world we're struggling to feed people. On the other side of the world, people are paying money to lose weight. I watch commercials on TV for weight-loss programs and I scream, "You want to lose weight—go to Africa! How about that? How about if you lose weight while you're helping people? Do you ever think about that? You'll feel good *and* different, too. You'll accomplish two powerful things at one time. I promise you, when you come back you will have learned so much. Your mind will be much clearer than when you left home."

Today, I cherish the value of the simple things. I meet people every day who have beautiful homes, sometimes several homes, cars, boats, jewels, but all they think about is getting more, as if that next thing they buy will finally bring them happiness and peace of mind. However, I don't need a diamond ring to make me happy. People say, oh, that's easy for you to say now that you can afford to buy what you want. But I don't want anything. The most valuable asset in life—other than life itself—is health. But people ruin their precious health worrying about all kinds of pointless little irritations—"Oh, here comes that bill, and another bill, and bills flying in from every direction, and . . . oh, how am I going to pay them all?" The U.S. is the wealthiest country in the world, yet everybody feels poor.

And more than bankrupt of money, everyone is bankrupt of time. Everybody's got no time. No time at all. "Get out of my way, man, I'm in a hurry!" The streets are packed with people rushing here and there and chasing God only knows what.

I *am* grateful that I've experienced both lives—the simple way and the fast way. But without growing up in Africa, I don't know if I would have learned to enjoy life the simple way. My childhood in Somalia shaped my personality forever, and has kept me from taking seriously trivial issues like success and fame that seem to obsess so many people. Frequently I'm asked, "How does it feel to be famous?"—and I just laugh. What does that mean, famous? I don't even know. All I know is that my way of thinking is an African way, and that will never change.

One of the greatest benefits of living in the West is peace, and I'm not sure how many people realize what a blessing that is. True, there is crime, but that is not the same thing as having a war raging around you. I have been thankful for shelter here and the opportunity to raise my baby in safety, because Somalia has seen constant fighting since rebels ousted Siad Barre in 1991. Rival tribes have fought for control ever since, and no one knows how many people have been killed. The beautiful city of white buildings that the Italian colonists built, Mogadishu, has been destroyed. Nearly every structure bears the marks of seven years of nonstop fighting, with buildings bombed or shot full of bullet holes. There is no longer any hint of order in the city—no government, no police, no schools.

It is depressing for me to know that my family has not escaped this fighting. My uncle Wolde'ab, my mother's brother who was so funny and looked so much like Mama, died in Mogadishu. He was standing by a window when his house was sprayed with gunfire. The entire building was shot full of holes, and a bullet came through the window and killed my uncle.

Even the nomadic people are affected now. When I saw my little brother, Ali, in Ethiopia, he had been shot also, and narrowly escaped getting killed. He was walking alone with his camels, when poachers ambushed him and shot him in the arm. Ali fell down and pretended to be dead, and the poachers made off with his entire herd.

When I saw my mother in Ethiopia, she told me she was still carrying a bullet in her chest after being caught in crossfire. My sister had taken her to the hospital in Saudi, but they said she was too old for them to operate. Surgery would be dangerous, and she might not survive. Yet, by the time I saw her, she seemed strong as a camel. She was Mama, tough as always, and cracking jokes about getting shot. I asked her if the bullet was still inside her, and she said, "Yeah, yeah, it's in there. I don't care. Maybe I melted it down by now."

These tribal wars, like the practice of circumcision, are brought about by the ego, selfishness, and aggression of men. I hate to say that, but it's true. Both acts stem from their obsession with their territory—their possessions—and women fall into that category both culturally and legally. Perhaps if we cut their balls off, my country would become paradise. The men would calm down and be more sensitive to the world. Without that constant surge of testosterone, there'd be no war, no killing, no thieving, no rape. And if we chopped off their private parts, and turned them loose to run around and either bleed to death or survive, maybe they could understand for the first time what they're doing to their women.

My goal is to help the women of Africa. I want to see them get stronger, not weaker, and the practice of FGM simply weakens them physically and emotionally. Since women are the backbone of Africa, and they do most of the work, I like to imagine how much they could accomplish if they weren't butchered as children and left to function maimed for the rest of their lives.

In spite of my anger over what has been done to me, I don't blame my parents. I love my mother and father. My mother had no say-so in my circumcision, because as a woman she is powerless to make decisions. She was simply doing to me what had been done to her, and what had been done to her mother, and her mother's mother. And my father was completely ignorant of the suffering he was inflicting on me; he knew that in our Somalian society, if he wanted his daughter to marry, she must be circumcised or no man would have her. My parents were both victims of their own upbringing, cultural practices that have continued unchanged for thousands of years. But just as we know today that we can avoid disease and death by vaccinations, we know that women are not animals in heat, and their loyalty has to be earned with trust and affection rather than barbaric rituals. The time has come to leave the old ways of suffering behind.

I feel that God made my body perfect the way I was born. Then man robbed me, took away my power, and left me a cripple. My womanhood was stolen. If God had wanted those body parts missing, why did he create them?

I just pray that one day no woman will have to experience this pain. It will become a thing of the past. People will say, "Did you hear, female genital mutilation has been outlawed in Somalia?" Then the next country, and the next, and so on, until the world is safe for all women. What a happy day that will be, and that's what I'm working toward. *In'shallah*, if God is willing, it will happen.

Join the Campaign to Eliminate FGM through

Waris Dirie Foundation
Millenium Tower, 24th Floor
Handelskai 94-96
1200 Vienna
Austria

Email: <u>waris@utanet.at</u>
Homepage: <u>www.waris-dirie-foundation.com</u>